iamm46

the interview

m-foddysix

iamm46: the interview by m-foddysix

Published by M46

ISBN: 9780578297200 (print)

Printed in USA

For my daughters, Bonolo, Mabi & Naledi. XOXO

For my co-author, my mother. Thanks for everything, including the information you've provided to make this book possible. Love you for eternity.

A.m.Dew, thanks for working through pain to ensure this book sees the light of day. You're super awesome. *That's for sure!*

Tumi Yukii, thanks for all your help.

Contents

Behind the scenes: Platinum VIP backstage pass

Hi there, M46, aka, M-Foddysix here, and welcome to my world, PlanetM46! I am back here catching up with my hosts, Dew and Sage, before we go on air for our first installment of our interview series. So make yourself comfortable as we journey through my childhood stories.

***

Dew: *[Pulling a baby-tasting-a-lemon face] Ew,* CHICKEN FEET! That is like, so disgusting. No offense Mrm46, but eating chicken feet is totally gross. This one time I saw my friend, Syd's mom eating those things. Yuck! It was so disturbing... like she was eating her own fingers, except they had four tiny fingers. Just google "chicken feet with nail polish" and you'll see what I'm talking about. Seriously, they really look like a girl's hands.

Sage: Oh, snap! Look M46, she ain't lying!

Me: Wow! That's so sick. *[Turning towards Dew]* But you still don't know whatcha missing!

Dew: Ugh! Just the thought of eating feet makes me wanna puke. *[Gagging]* Can we talk about something else, please? I'm like, totally grossed out right now.

Me: Okay, we can talk about Mr. Oink Oink's feet... Do you eat those?

Dew: No, I don't... eat... dead... animals' transportation! I think I'm gonna get sick. *[Races to the restroom]*

Sage: *[Confused]* Animal transportation? Makes no sense.

Me: She means feet, dude—

Sage: I knew that.

Me: Bet ya did. Anyway, how about you, do you eat animal feet?

Sage: Err... M-Foddysix, I have eaten a lot of stuff in my life, but eating dead hooves, dead feet, or dead walking finger-toes is totally *ewgusting*!

Me: "Ewgusting?"

Sage: "EW" plus "DISGUSTING." Super disgusting.

[Dew returns]

Dew: You knew what, Sage? What y'all talkin' bout now?

Me: *[Teasing]* Uh... was just telling Sage here about my favorite dessert.

Dew: Oh, yum. What is it?

Me: Frozen octopus brains.

Dew: Yuck! FROZEN OCTO WHAT?

[Dew races back to the restroom]

Me: *[Frowning]* Why does she keep running to the restroom?

Sage: Cos she's easily grossed out. Err... M46, think you can hook me up with some of those brains?

Me: Sage, I was just joking. There are no frozen octopus brains.

Sage: Aw, man. I always wanted to try some.

***

Mrs. Fartpigg, the stage director, walks backstage and hooks a cordless mic on my tee.

Mrs. Fartpigg: Guest, please say something... anything.

Me: *[Playfully]* Something. Anything.

Mrs. Fartpigg: *[Adjusting a mic from a controller]* Okay silly man, your mic is all set.

Me: Thank you, Mrs. Pigfart.

Mrs. Fartpigg: It's Mrs. Fartpigg, not Pigfart!

Me: Oh, my apologies, Mrs. Fartpigg. Didn't realize that *fart* comes before *pigg. [Whispering to Sage]* Why can't it just be Pigfart? Sounds better.

Sage: Yeah, I know, right?! Bad kids call her that behind her back.

Mrs. Fartpigg: You realize your mic is still on. And Sage, you owe me some names.

Sage: But I didn't do anything!

***

On stage, theater students are busy setting up for the interview. Dew and Sage sit on the couch on the stage while I remain behind the curtains. Mrs. Fartpigg checks their microphone levels and cues the camera crew.

Mrs. Fartpigg: Cam-one, close-up on Dew, please.... Perfect! Cam-two, fix a close-up on Sage.... Great! Cam-three, gimme wide... and stop. Alright super-team, we are ready to roll. On three, two, one... and... ACTION!"

—the interview

Dew: You ready, bruh?

Sage: Born ready!

Dew: Okay, let's do this! Good morning, everyone. Welcome to another episode of "Let's Set the Records Straight with Dew and Sage," the only middle school morning announcement show that leaves nothing to the imagination! Today we are super excited to have a special guest on the show. He's our very own, and one of our favorites.

[Curiosity is building up]

Ladies and gentlemen, boys and girls, please put your hands together and help me welcome the one, the only, Mr. M-forty-s-i-i-i-x!

I walk out and the kids immediately lose their minds. Cheers fill the cafeteria - kids are whistling and clapping.

Students: Yay! It's Mr. M-forty-s-i-i-i-x! Agent M-forty-s-i-i-i-x! Mr. Grinch! Squeaky Voice!

I wave and blow kisses and throw hand-hearts back at 'em. Now I can't help but swing my hips side to side, "Flossing."

Me: C'mon everybody, bust a move!

They all go wild again, swinging and twisting their hips in jubilation.

Student: Yay, I like this guy!

[We do a few Fortnite dances]

Students: Do the Orange Justice! Now Dab! Do 'The Hype'! Do 'The Fresh'! Jubilation!

Student: I told you, he's so cool. He's the G.O.A.T!

Student 2: I know him. He was my sub in fifth grade!

Student: Yeah, he played soccer with us at recess. Best sub ever!

Slowly the roars fade. I take a seat and Mrs. Fartpigg cues Cam-four.

"Cam-four, fix a close-up on the guest... and stay! Thank you."

Dew: Let's hear it again for Mr. M-forty-s-i-i-x!

[Cheers follow, then Dew continues]

He's here today to let us into Planet M46 through his #1, Coast to Coast Times bestseller, *iamm46: the interview.* He's promised to tell it all. From growing up in South Africa to his experiences right here in America. He's also promised a sneak peek of his upcoming national tour featuring stand-up comedy, book review and signing on different campuses across America...

[Claps and cheers erupt again]

... Wait, I'm not finished y'all. And I quote, "For the love y'all have shown me, I've titled my tour, *Discovered by my Students!*" Isn't that *like,* sooo cool?

[Loud cheers continue]

By the way, I had the pleasure of skimming through the first copy of this must-read earlier. You guys, I promise it is jam-packed with hilarious stories; you'll laugh until you turn blue in the face. Okay, who's ready to get a copy?

Students: Me, me, me, me...

Dew: Okay, y'all can buy copies in the library after the assembly. And buy one for your siblings, too.

Me: Thanks, Dew. You are the *bestest, ever-est there-ist.*

Dew: You are welcome. And welcome to the show.

Me: Thank you. It's so nice to be here.

Dew: Super excited! Alright Sage, take it away.

Sage: Thanks, Dew. Okay everyone, let's get this road on the show.

[Laughter fills the cafeteria]

Dew: *[Whispering]* Sage, it's "show on the road." Not—

Sage: I knew that. Just warming up the crowd.

[Dew shakes her head]

Sage: Okay, everybody let's get this show on the road. This is how this interview is gonna flow. Dew and I will ask M46 some Qs. Then we'll open the floor and have Mr. Curl pass the mic for y'all to ask Qs. Cool?

[Cheers follow]

Dew: Alright y'all, kick back, relax and enjoy the ride as we burn through our Friday assembly hour with the one... the only....... Mr. M-forty-s-i-i-i-i-x!

[Cheering continues]

Dew: They sure love you. You're like a celeb here!

Sage: Yeah, a rock star sub.

Me: *[Blowing more kisses]* I don't know about all that, but I love 'em back.

Dew: It's so great to see you again.

Sage: Yeah, and as a surprise, too. We just found out like an hour ago.

Dew: Yeah man, like literally.

Me: Hey, that's how I roll, y'all. But, seriously, I'm thrilled to see y'all again, too. Uh... before we get started, I'd like to spit a few things out, if that's alright.

Dew: That's alright with me.

Me: Cool. Sup, everyone! I'm super excited to be with y'all this morning. It feels so great to be back here. Please give it up for Dew and Sage! These guys are the rock stars of the middle school morning announcements.

[Cheers and claps ensue. After a brief pause, I continue]

To all the district's staff: Thank you for the great work you do for our students.

A big thank you to the amazing teachers. It's an honor to work with, and sub for such awesome educators. Americas' finest! Y'all are the real superheroes minus capes. Thank you for the opportunities to work with your students.

To the admin staff: Your hard work and commitment to excellence doesn't go unnoticed. Thank you for the warm welcomes you give to me and other subs each morning.

Other staff: Thank you for keeping our schools safe, clean and functional.

I'd also like to thank the parents for your wonderful children. A special thank you to those of you who've showered me with kind words of gratitude on IG or via emails to teachers. Thanks to those who have waited to meet me after school and said, "Thank you for putting smiles on our kiddos' faces." I don't deserve the credit, but they're all heartfelt.

[Unfolding my note]

And now to the greatest friends I've ever had. This is a personal appreciation letter to you guys, my students. My inspiration. The coolest kids in the world!

No language has enough words to express my deepest gratitude.

Thank you for receiving me with excitement and enthusiasm - the "YESes" I hear when you find me in your classrooms. Thank you for all the tangible gifts you've given Me: the wonderful notes, inspiring letters and drawings. They fill my heart with delight.

Thank you for the stage and the audience you've given me to share my stories. Your classrooms are where I became myself. It's a place where I get courage to dream big dreams again.

Thank you for inspiring me to be the best I can be. I'm thankful for the courage you've given me to challenge myself to reach for the summit.

You've given me more than I could've ever imagined. You've given me a reason to live life to the fullest.

And you know what makes it so special? Is that you guys don't even know it! You don't know how much impact you've made in my life. And for that, you'll forever hold a special place in my heart.

[Dew wipes off tears]

Sorry Dew, didn't mean to get you *emo* there. Okay, last but not least, a big fat monstrous thank you for discovering me – my comedy. I'm proud to tell the world I was discovered by y'all.

Thank you all.

Signed: Mrm46, Mr.M- Foddysix, Mr. M-Foddysumtin, Mr. 2.0, Mr. Grinch, Mr. Spaghetti, Mr. M&M, Mr. Fortnite, Mr. Squeaky Voice, and all the other names you've given me.

***

Dew: Thank you again for dropping in, Mrm46. It's such a pleasure to have you here! Wait, I almost forgot. Today is your birthday! A big happy birthday to you!

Me: Thank you, Dew.

Dew: You're welcome. Now a ton of kids have been arguing about your name. Did it change at midnight? Are you now Mrm47?

Me: Yes and No. But let's talk about that next Friday when we unpack book two.

Dew: Cool. Okay, before kick off the interview, let's talk a bit about why you decided to write this book now, and the genre. I think it's really interesting how you combined two genres.

—why this book, why now?

Dew: Okay, what is a fictionalized memoir? Why did you choose to blend the genres? And why did you write it in an interview format?

Me: Great Qs, Dew. Um... So, a fictionalized memoir is basically nonfiction and fiction coexisting in a book. You know, part factual, part creativity. That's the simplest definition. As for blending the genres, I did it because it allowed me to explore my creative side. Create characters and watch them come to life.

Basically, this allowed me to tell true stories and, occasionally, spice them with products of my imagination. And the format, I really wanted to write something different. I wanted to make you guys, my readers, part of the total experience.

Dew: Well, I'm glad you did, because it's just so cool. And the few dialogues I read earlier in the anthropomorphism, especially the lines by Jojo, the "talking" donkey were *mad* funny!

Sage: Anthropomo who? And who's Jojo, the talking donkey?

Dew: Read the book and you'll know.

Sage: I am starting today, so it's okay to gimme a heads up.

Dew: Nice try, dude. *[Turning towards me]* What was the hardest part of putting all these stories together?

Me: Mixing the genres. So, I had written this anthropomorphism play featuring two donkey siblings, Jojo and Grace, and I wanted to include their story in the book. So I did. It wasn't easy, though. I mostly struggled with switching between back and forth. You know, finding the right place to switch and still keep consistency.

Dew: Interesting! That's what I thought of when I was leafing through that chapter. Okay, Sage, do you have a Q for Mrm46?

Sage: Okay M46, remember the first time you told us a funny story and every time you came back we asked for more?

Me: Yeah, I remember that. 'Twas like you guys were calling each other and saying, "Hey, Mrm46 is our sub tomorrow."

"Oh, Cool. Ask him to tell y'all a funny story."

Dew: Uh... actually, we kinda did.

Sage: Do other kids do it, too?

Me: All the time. I had one kid say, "Hey Mr. Foddysumtin, if you won't tell, we won't tell. You know, we could just skip math today and listen to your stories." She was tryna cut a deal to get out of doing school work.

Spoiler alert: Never happened.

Dew: We always had *sooo* much fun with you in class.

Sage: Yeah, you made school fun for us.

Me: Thank you guys. I had fun, too. You guys were the best. And still are!

Dew: *[Smiling big]* Awesome! Okay, back to my original Q: Why this book, why now?

Me: Well, the short answer is it was out of necessity. As you know, I sub in a lot of schools and because of that, I've taught thousands of kids. I love it, though. I get to choose where to go; the group of kids to hang out with for the day.

Dew: Now that is just so cool. I wish I could just wake up and choose a school to go to. That would be like *sooo* amazing cos I'd make a ton of friends.

Me: I know, right? I like that it allows me to interact with a ton of kids. Like, in elementary schools, for instance, I get to hang out with an average of 120 kids in a single day. The number is slightly higher for middle schools — plus or minus, 160 kids.

So if you multiply that by five, you end up with a whopping 600 elementary school kids and 800 middle schoolers in one week. And when you multiply that by four weeks in a month, I teach anywhere between 2400 to 3200 kids, depending on the grade levels.

Sage: Wow, that's a *lot* of kids!

Me: Yes, the numbers are astronomical, but it wasn't always like that. When I first started, I only taught regular classes in elementary schools. But as I moved to more schools, I met more kids. And the more kids I met; the more stories I shared. And more kids asked me to come back. I did that for a while, but after being to so many schools, it became impossible to keep up with my promises.

So I switched to specials and taught five or six classes per day instead. But with more kids, the requests grew. I'd literally spend each day repeating the same stories and answering the same Qs over and over again.

Dew: Cool, but what does this have to do with my Q?

Me: Everything. Think about it.

[Dew and Sage put their thinking caps on]

Dew: *[Bulb goes off]* Oh, I get it now! So you basically killed two birds with one stone.

Sage: What? Why did you do that? You shouldn't kill birds, M-Foddysix!

Dew: Sage, it means he—

Sage: I knew that. Just wanted to see if you knew it, too.

Dew: Whatever, Sage!

Me: Yeah, whatever, Sonnyboy. Anyway, I penned it so I wouldn't have to repeat myself every day.

Dew: That's awesome, but does it mean you won't tell us stories in person anymore? Cos that would suck!

Me: No, I'll still treat you guys, just not on heavy rotation.

Dew: *Yas!* Okay, I think this would be the perfect time to tell us about yourself. Maybe you can start off with where you were born, you know, tell us about your childhood.

part one
the beginning

1 childhood stories: who is m46?

aka, m-foddysix

So my mother, the funniest person I know, tells a story about my birth and how I got sick shortly after. She begins the story with a fight we had hours before my arrival.

[Part 1: told to me when I was 5 years old]

"It was a freezing winter day. I'd just lit our coal stove when the sharpest pain zapped throughout my belly.

"Argh! Would you stop kicking me, you ungrateful, unborn child? I'm not your soccer ball, you know!

"Before I could yell again, you kicked as if you'd heard me.

"Listen to me, you little nuisance, this will be the last time you kick me!

"But my words fell on deaf ears. Instead, you kicked and kicked like it was a penalty shootout. Then, in the middle of that, my water broke."

"Uh-oh mommy, you should be careful because when you break your water you'll be in trouble with *Koko [grandma].*"

"No, son, it was you."

"But I wasn't carrying the bucket. You're trying to blame me. Hmph!"

"Know what? I'll explain it later. But for now, just know there was no bucket of water. It was time for your birth.

"Anyway, my cousin rushed me to Bara hospital. After seeing the doctor, he immediately prepared for a C-Section delivery."

"What is See-suction?"

"C-Section is a surgery doctors use to deliver babies."

"Why?"

"Well, for many reasons, but in your case, it was your positioning. Normally, babies move into a head-first position towards birth..."

"Why?"

"So that the head comes out of the tummy first. But you, naughty boy, you'd flipped to a foot-first position. You were trying to come out with your feet first."

"Oh, now I remember. I was doing a flip, then a bicycle kick, but I got stuck. So I stayed like that so when it was time to come out I'd be on my feet, ready to play soccer with my friends."

"Really?"

"Yes, you don't remember, mommy? I wanted to play with my friends because in your tummy I didn't have anyone to play with. Other babies have a sister to play with and they come out together holding hands. And they're called twins."

"Who told you twins are born holding hands?"

"Nobody. I just know because I see grandpa and *Koko* spending time together and holding hands all the time. That means they're twins; they came out together."

"No, your grandparents are not twins. They hold hands because they're married."

"Well, I'm getting married, too, so when I go back into your tummy, I won't be by myself again. It was boring."

"You're going back into my tummy?"

"Yes. *Koko* said when you die, you go back to where you came from. So I came from your tummy. That means I'm gonna go back into your tummy."

"Okay, can I continue now?"

"Yes, mommy."

"Good! Once the doctor was ready to cut me open..."

"Noooo, stop, mommy. I don't like him cutting up your tummy. He almost cut me, too."

"How do you know that?"

"Well, I saw the knife because I was looking at it like this *[Frowning],* so I did a backflip because he was gonna cut off my hand. But when I was not looking, he cut off my tail."

"You have a wild imagination, son. People don't have tails."

"That's because doctors cut them off in the belly."

"Who told you... never mind. Anyway, the doctor cut me open and after a few minutes, you were born."

"Yay! Clap for me, mommy. Now, let's get some chocolate. It's my birthday."

"We don't have any chocolate."

"Yes, we do. Let me show you."

[So you went to the cabinet and brought back some Brooklax].

"Now, can I please have two pieces?"

"No, you can only eat one."

"But the last time when you were not here, I ate five pieces."

"What? Who gave 'em to you?"

"I got 'em by myself. No one was in the house, and I was looking for something and then I saw chocolate. I wasn't looking for it, okay, mommy. But when I saw it there, I thought *Koko* had left it for me. So I ate it up. *Shhhh!* don't tell Mae, okay? I spent the whole day running to the toilet. First, I was running, and then I stopped. I was trying to hold it, but it was too late. Then I sat on the toilet the whole day because my tummy was hurting."

"That's because you were sick."

"Mommy, no one gets sick from eating sweets [candy]."

"Listen to me, laxatives are not sweets. Never do that again, do you understand?"

"Yes. I don't like your story anymore."

"Don't be sad. But I mean it. Come here... *tickle, tickle!*"

"Hahaha, stop, mommy!"

[Part 2: told to 13 years later]

After repeating the first part, she continued where she had left off.

"Oh, I remember that day like it was yesterday. After you were born, you almost gave me a heart attack. See, normal babies cry after birth, but you didn't. So naturally I got worried. I thought you were a stillborn. To make it worse, the nurse rushed out of the room with you.

Doctor, what's wrong? Why is she running away with my baby? Is my baby okay?"

"Yes, Ms. Moeng, he's fine. The nurse is going to clean him up and she'll bring him right back to you."

"Thank you, doctor."

***

"Minutes later, the nurse brought you back — all cleaned and wrapped up in a nice cozy blankie."

"Here's your baby boy, ma'am. Congratulations!" she said as she placed you in my arms.

"Aww! Thank you, nurse. But next time you wanna scare somebody like that, running with somebody's baby, have some decency and put some clothes on that thing.

"Everybody in that room laughed so hard."

"Laughed at that thing? What thing?"

"Would you let me finish my story?"

"As you wish, Mother. I'll just pretend you're talking about a thing, *not* me."

"Good. Anyway, I was excited to see my baby. But when I looked closer, two things caught my attention right away: Your head was extremely small—"

"Of course, babies have small heads."

"Yes, that's true, but yours was unusually small, son. I immediately worried that kids would tease you, calling you an ostrich head boy."

"Mother, you know that I'm still here, hearing everything you're saying."

[Ignoring me] "I had to think of a plan to hide your head from those mean kids. After thinking about it for about two seconds, I got a brilliant idea."

"And what was the brilliant idea?"

"A helmet.

"A HELMET?"

"Yes, a helmet. An ostrich-head-sized helmet. But then it hit me. I'd never seen an ostrich wearing a helmet. Son, have you ever seen an ostrich wearing a helmet?"

"No, Mother. I have never seen an ostrich wearing a helmet because ostriches don't ride motorcycles or play American football. Ostriches don't ride skateboards or go skiing. Ostriches are super-sized monster chickens, and chickens don't wear helmets."

"Well, that's too bad."

[After a brief pause]

“Was it really that tiny?”

“Itty bitty. Alright, let me help you understand. Think of a doll... like Barbie. Now, think of Barbie with her head snatched off. Can you see her headless body with just the piece that attaches to the head? That’s how you looked. The tiny knob was your head.”

“Wow! I can see why you were terrified.”

“Terrified!? I wasn't I just didn’t want to be on the front page of a newspaper, under a title, ‘A normal mother gives birth to an abnormal baby with an ostrich head.’”

“Hahaha, very funny, Mother.”

“I was also worried you’d not have enough brain to understand anything in school. So I moved to Plan B.”

“Ooh, Plan B, huh! What was Plan B?”

“A beanie. I thought if I put ten beanies on your head, they’d make it look bigger.”

“Mother!”

“What? I had to do something about it. Anyway, after putting the first one, you disappeared.”

[Excitedly] “Ahh, you mean I had superpowers. I always knew I was born a ninja-spy-superhero.”

“Nope, sorry to burst your bubble. You didn’t. The beanie had swallowed your head. The whole thing. And with clothes covering your entire body, you looked like a stuffed-animal pillow. And you’d make these tiny sounds, which made you look and sound like a cat stuck in a sack.

"Haha."

"The beanie experiment became our favorite *hide-and-seek* game. I'd put it on your head, and as soon as it swallowed you, you'd cry. Then I'd remove it, and you'd laugh hard."

"Mother, I demand an apology. Entertaining yourself at my expense is child abuse."

[Ignoring me] "You know what else I worried about? Your eyes. You only had these tiny dots under your eyebrows. So I worried that you'd run into things as soon as you started walking."

"And what did you do, put flashlights on the side of my head?"

"No, son, there was nowhere to glue them, and your ears couldn't handle the weight. But I came up with another brilliant idea. I searched for a doctor who could give you Coke-bottle glasses. Unfortunately, I couldn't find anyone who specialized in ostrich glasses. So I moved to Plan C: make the glasses myself."

"What do you mean, make 'em yourself? Wait a minute, Uh-uh. No. Uh-uh. Please tell me you were not thinking of doing what I'm thinking you were!"

"I'm not in your head, but I was going to cut the bottoms of soda bottles and make you some glasses."

"Okay, let me get this straight. First, you were gonna put a helmet on my head, not because I'd been riding a motorcycle or playing football, but to hide my head from the public."

"Yes."

"Then, you were gonna put Coke-bottle glasses on my face, not because I was blind, but because my eyes were tiny?"

"Yes.'"

"And when you didn't find an ostrich-head-size glass maker because none exists, and because ostriches don't wear glasses, you bought two Coke bottles and attempted to cut them yourself."

"Yes."

"So what happened to the soda?"

"I drank it."

"Well, did you at least give me some?"

"No, son, I didn't want you to have a brain freeze. It was too cold for an ostrich brain."

"Haha. Let's just say you were successful - you had these so-called *windows* made, didn't you think they would've been too heavy for an 'ostrich neck?'"

"Of course I did, son. But that's where neck braces and casts come in."

"Wait, a minute! So now I was gonna walk around with a helmet on my head, windows on my face and a cast on my neck. What kind of mother does that?"

"Stop judging me. Any mother would've done just that for her blind child with a peanut head. I wanted you to have a normal life. I didn't want school kids to call you blind-ostrich-head-boy, when you ran into them."

"There you go again, talking like I wasn't a normal person."

"Do you think you were? Do you think anyone with a tiny head like that can be normal?"

"You realize that you're the only person in the entire world who thinks like that, Mother?"

"Really? What are the other people thinking?"

"I don't know. But you're also the only one who'd call her son blind-ostrich-sized-head-boy."

"You mean, those mean kids never called you that? Praise the lord. My prayers worked."

***

Dew: [Laughing] A helmet for an ostrich-head-sized boy...with Coke bottom glasses? That's too funny. Sorry, Mrm46, but she's too funny!

Me: Hey, watch yourself. That's not funny.

Dew: Sorry, but this is too much!

Me: Anyway, after roasting me, she had a sudden mood swing.

—a very sick boy

"I remember the day you fell sick. Your body started burning with fever. Then the constant throwing up began and nothing stayed in your tummy. The doctor got the fever under control, but you started fainting. Your sudden health decline changed our lives."

"Wow! What did you do?"

"Your grandparents suggested we join them in the village, but I declined. I didn't think it was a good idea. We needed to be in a township or city. A place with reliable transportation and hospitals. So we remained in Soweto, and I did laundry for money to help with your care."

"Thanks for caring for me, mother. Thank you for being the best!"

"You are welcome, son."

"What happened next?"

"One day a stranger showed up–someone visiting an old lady I was doing odd jobs for. After hearing about your condition, she swore that this young doctor would heal you. I didn't need further convincing. I got the address, and we got on the road right away.

We stayed the night with my aunty, *Koko's* sister, and her family. No one slept that night: You stayed up, shedding tears as usual, and all the adults took turns monitoring you. We all sang nursery songs as you silently wept. *Thula thula nana, didimala. Didimala nana, didimala* (Hush baby, please hush).

"Please, baby, stay with me. Help has come. The morning will be here soon, and you'll be alright," I whispered those words into your ears all night long.

"At last, the morning came. It was still dark outside, but with my auntie leading the way, we marched like it was midday. After walking a bit, a taxi picked us up. When auntie told the driver where we were going, his face lit up. He praised the doctor for the entire trip. All the while, you kept your tiny eyes open and squirmed as he went on and on. It was almost as if you knew that help had finally come. Maybe you did. After all, I had flooded your ears with that promise the entire night before.

"He's a miracle worker. Your son will be fine by the end of the day!" The driver offered his last praise as he drove off.

At 6:50 a.m., the man hailed as a "miracle worker" arrived. He was a soft-spoken man with an average size build. Face full of beard. Energetic and full of life. As soon as he saw us, he walked over and inquired about your symptoms. After briefing him, he began examining you. Though he didn't say you'd be healed by the end of the day, as the taxi driver had claimed, my tension eased up. I immediately felt like my prayers had been answered. I felt you were in good care and he cared genuinely.

"Don't worry, ma'am, I'm going to take good care of your son. I have treated many children with similar conditions and all of them recovered within days or weeks," he said as he took you to the exam room. After examining you, he told us you were dehydrated. Your White Blood Cell count was low, which made your tiny body unable to fend off diseases. You also had ulcers in your tummy, which caused the throwing up.

"He began your treatment immediately by increasing your body fluid intake and catching you up on your shots."

"Did he heal me the same day?"

"No, but we stayed with aunties for your follow up treatment.

In the following days, you began making steady progress. For the first time in months, I saw a ray of hope on your face: you smiled. Within weeks, you had made an impressive improvement. The fainting was gone. You were devouring food like a pig, and your body weight was back to normal.

I was thrilled that my little blind ostrich had turned into a piglet, feeding without throwing up. I moved from washing two to three napkins (diapers) a day to cleaning up to ten. Luckily, in those days we used cloth napkins, otherwise you'd have spent the first two years of your life sitting and sleeping on the potty."

"Mother, can you stop joking?"

"After two weeks, he discharged you. But we remained there for a few more months until I was completely satisfied. The following year, before your first birthday, we went back to Soweto. From that moment onwards, you never got sick again."

"Awesome! Did we ever see my superhero doc again?"

"No, son, we didn't. By the time I tried, he'd moved to another part of the country."

"Aw, man!"

“Sometimes people come into our lives, do what they are supposed to do, and disappear.”

“Anyway, thanks, doc! Thank you for giving me another shot at life.”

***

Dew: Wow, he was just awesome. Thank you, Doctor Amazing!

Sage: Yeah, thanks Doc, otherwise we wouldn’t have known M46.

Me: True. I’m forever grateful for his intervention.

Dew: And your mom, she’s really hilarious. Now we know where your sense of humor comes from.

Me: Yeah, I got it from my mama. She’s so funny, and she never wastes an opportunity for a good belly laugh.

Dew: I loved how she lightened up the story with her sense of humor. I really enjoyed it. Please tell us more of her stories!

Me: Sure. Apparently, when I was little, my eyes introduced me to something really, really weird. Being the last born in my family, I’d not lay my eyes on such a fascinating mystery until I was five or six years old.

2 life before school — the watermelon

a mystery in the belly

"One weekend when I was home on leave, you went to play with Mae. A few minutes later, *we* heard you screaming from the gate, talking about cutting somebody's belly open. '*Koko*, get a knife! We have to cut Mae's mom's belly!' You ran straight to the kitchen and grabbed a butter knife and continued screaming, 'I saw it!'

"You saw what, son?"

"A watermelon, and it's going to kill her."

"Okay, slow down. What are you talking about? How's a watermelon going to do that to a person?"

"Because she swallowed it! We have to cut her tummy open and get it out!"

"Your grandmother (*Koko*) and I couldn't help it but fell on the ground. It was so funny because you were convinced she'd actually swallowed a whole watermelon."

While we were rolling on the ground laughing, you tried to run out of the door with the butter knife in your hand. Right then I knew you were gonna cut my cousin with that knife, so we took the knife from you.

In the next few minutes, you seemed calm. But then, while we were not watching, you grabbed another knife and sneaked out of the door. By the time we realized you were gone, you were already halfway flying to Mae's house."

"You better catch that boy before he hurts someone with that knife!" Koko said as we chased you down. We ran after you, but we couldn't catch up. You were so fast, which was so funny because you were so short. I remember at one point not seeing you, but the dust billowing behind you.

"When I finally caught up with you, you were banging on their door, 'Mae's mom, open the door and come outside! I have a knife to cut your belly and get the watermelon out. Open the door!'

I grabbed the knife and sat you on the porch. *Koko* caught up, too, and tried to clear the confusion for you.

"Grandson, Mae's mom, didn't swallow a watermelon. It's her baby."

"It's a baby watermelon? We have to get it out, *Koko*. Nobody should have a baby watermelon growing in their tummy."

"No, it's not a baby watermelon; it's her baby."

"No matter how much she tried to convince you, you insisted it was a watermelon. Your mind believed that your grandmother (who carried me in her belly, and me, who carried you in my belly) didn't know what we were talking about. Only you knew."

"No, *Koko*, you don't know. It's a watermelon. I saw it. I really did! I know a watermelon, *Koko*, even when it is hiding in Mae's tummy."

"No, grandson, what you saw is a baby. She's going to have a baby soon."

Still, you were not convinced. In fact, you stopped eating watermelon that day.

"Okay mommy, but I don't eat watermelons anymore."

"Why not?"

"Because if I swallow the seed, it will grow in my tummy and turn into a baby. I don't want a baby in my tummy. I am a boy."

"Child, you will not have a baby in your tummy!"

Still, you were not totally convinced. You began questioning how babies lived in the tummy.

—but it can't swim!

One day we were at the hospital for a check-up, and you wouldn't stop staring at this lady in the waiting room. Suddenly, your silly thoughts returned.

"Are you sure it's not a watermelon, mommy?"

"No, not again." Then I got an idea. "Why don't you ask her? Go on... ask her."

"Nothing could stop you until you had cracked that mystery. So you walked to the lady and asked, 'Excuse me, is it a watermelon or a baby in your tummy?' The woman couldn't help but burst out laughing. But then, suddenly, a labor pain attack interrupted her uncontrollable laugh. Within seconds, she'd moved from laughing to yelling. That scared you, and you ran past me and hid behind a chair.

Once she'd calmed down, you walked back to her and continued interrogating her. She assured you there were no fruits or vegetables stuck in her tummy. Still not totally convinced, you walked away. With a new imagination.

I asked you what she told you, but you said she didn't know what she was talking about. Then you sat at the table and pretended you were reading a newspaper. You couldn't read yet, but you made-up words. You were so convinced you were reading the news for everyone in the waiting room. People gathered to listen to the "star news anchor." I sat there watching you and thinking you must be destined for stardom.

For a while, everything was going well. Then you flipped the page and saw "something disturbing." Suddenly, you were quiet. Then you made an announcement: "Listen everyone, there's been a terrible accident. The city bus has overturned."

One of your concerned audience members walked over to you to see the tragic accident (printed in the newspaper). Then she returned to inform everyone. They all fell on the ground laughing and called out to you. "Professor, your newspaper is upside down. Turn it the other way."

After turning it the correct way, you realized there was no accident, so you joined everybody laughing. But suddenly something went wrong; you started crying and everybody stopped laughing, thinking they were hurting your feelings.

"Why are you crying, professor?" They asked.

"The baby can't swim!" You ran to me, screaming. We were all confused. Then you walked back to the lady and snatched her water bottle.

"I'm so sorry ma'am! What did you do that for?" apologize to the lady!

"No, because she's gonna drown her baby!"

"Everyone started looking at each other and asking questions and shrugging shoulders. Nobody knew what was in your head."

"Why are you saying that?"

"Because the baby can't swim. He's going to drown!"

"When you said that, everyone couldn't help it but started laughing hard again. Including the lady. But in the middle of it, she got another labor pain and started screaming. "*Argh!*

Somebody get my husband. Help! Ooh, I'm gonna hurt him... he did this to me!"

Those words didn't help with the situation. If anything, they only helped fuel your suspicion: in your eyes, she was a bad lady who just tried to drown her unborn child, and now she's threatening to hurt her husband, too.

"Was I right? Did she hurt her husband?"

"Boy, she didn't mean it. It was labor pains making her talk like that."

"Oh, but what happened to her baby?"

"I don't know. When we left the hospital, she was in labor. I'm sure she gave birth, and they were both just fine.

***

Dew: *[Laughing hard]* I'm sorry, Professor Upside Down, but the city bus was overturned? That is so funny! I can't stop. Okay... Okay *[Taking a deep breath and fanning her face with her palms]* Okay, when did you... *[Continues to laugh]*... I'm sorry, MrM46, but this is too much.

Sage: That was wild, M46—

Dew: *[Interrupting]*—And the knife... were you gonna cut her belly, Doctor See-Suction?

Me: Hey I was tryna save a life.

Dew: With a butter knife?!

Sage: *[Laughing]* And how about, everyone is sitting on their heads!

Me: *[Playfully]* Hey, stop laughing at me. I was just a kid.

Dew: Sorry, professor... Upside Down! Any more stories from your mom?

Me: Know what? Her fifteen minutes of fame ends now. Tryna steal my spotlight. Thank you very much, Mother, but I'll take it from here!

Dew: Aww man, I am gonna miss her narration. Anyway, let's chug along. Tell us more of your childhood stories.

3 stuck behind the walls of boredom

the king of do-nothing

I am seven but I am not in school yet. All the kids my age started school last year, but I didn't. Maybe I'll join them next year. But until then, I stay home and spend my mornings with members of Senior Citizens Hot Tea Club [SCHTC], aka, Old People Club [OPC]. I call it SCHTC or OPC because they get together and drink hot tea in the heat and talk all day long.

If you ask me, this arrangement is not good for any of us. For one, they're getting too old because they *do nothing* but drink hot tea all day. Then, there's this forgetfulness business that's going on - I literally have to remind them of everything. And then, on top of that, they can't see or hear well anymore. I have to help *Koko* put the string in the needle all day long. As if that wasn't touture enough, but I have to keep repeating myself or scream when I talk to grandpa. On top of all that, I have to boil water every time another member comes over. This is not healthy!

I really think they need to do something better with their lives. You know, if it was up to me, I'd have bussed all of them to elementary school two years ago. At least there, the teacher would beat them with a stick if they forget stuff, and that would help them not forget anything.

***

Oh, I almost forgot! So, if you're wondering why I am not in school, you're not alone. I've been trying to get some answers myself. See, every time I ask my mother why she'd "waste my time like that" she won't give me a straight answer.

"Mother, why didn't I start school with kids my age? What was that all about, wasting my time and stuff?"

"I don't know, son. You know I work in the city. It's your grandparents' responsibility since you live with them."

See what I mean? Once again, she's just placed the blame on my grands, who are three hundred years old. Okay, that's an exaggeration. They are in their seventies, and people at that age don't always remember who their grandkids are. So how could they have remembered to register me at school?

Anyway, let's get something straight here: I'm not mad or anything. I know it sounds like I'm complaining about this whole "wasting time thingy," but between me and you, I'm really not. I think school is a great idea. But I think staying at home is *awesomer*. I am happy with an extra year of freedom: no jumping out of bed five days a week and running to school, no homework, and most importantly, no corporal punishment. I have it made.

But as much as I am happy to be home, there's one thing that spoils the fun: loneliness. I am stuck behind the walls of boredom. I am a king with no one in the castle to entertain *my majesty*: no jesters to have me rolling on the floor. No fiddlers on the roof to serenade me with some of the finest hip-hop jams. Not even a Barbie doll to shave her hair bald for amusement.

I, the king of doing nothing, literally have to entertain myself. Now that's *un-king-ly!* What good is a kingdom if the king gets bored, and there's nobody to entertain him? The king has to wait for those snot-faced, cootie super-spreaders to return from school. That's totally unacceptable. Something has to be done. And done right away. So, since I can't cancel school, I'm gonna pay the principal a visit and have a little chit chat. Please come with me.

***

"*Err...* excuse me, school principal, I'd like to have a word with you, if you don't mind."

"Look who's here! Are you ready to join us?"

"No, but I think you should release these kids at ten o'clock because that's when I wake up, and I need people to play with." I cut to the chase.

Okay, you'd think a principal, a learned member of society, would understand that boredom leads to loneliness, and loneliness leads to stress, and stress kills, right? Wrong! She doesn't. She's totally against my great idea. *Argh*, principals just don't understand!

Well, I guess I made the presentation about myself. I should have said something like, "Those cootie super-spreaders are too young to stay gone that long. Please release them at 10 a.m. sharp. Thank you very much."

No doubt this would've been a game-changer. [Pause] Wait a minute! There's one more thing I can do. The after-school bell just rang. Let's check with these snotty faces and have a little chit chat on the way home.

***

"Hi everyone, I have called this meeting because I have something important to say. You all need to quit school, or at least cut classes every day and keep me company."

[No answer]

"Hello? Are you people deaf? Is that what school is doing to you? Okay, listen, if you quit, you'll wake up at a decent hour, have no homework, and no more corporal punishment. Just like me."

[Still, no answer]

These snot faces are too chicken. *Argh*, I am so devastated right now! I thought they were my friends, but clearly school has turned them against me. *Argh*!

This is why I hate week days. I like weekends better because kids my age don't have to be held hostage in school. They stay home, come to my house and keep me company. Now, that is king-ly.

—self-entertain

If it were up to me, every day would be a weekend. Wouldn't you like that? Anyway, right now I have no choice but to be creative. Explore my mind. I don't have toys to play with, so I push bricks and pretend they're cars. Big bricks are like monster trucks and city buses, and the tiny ones are anything from a Cadillac to a Ferrari.

This is how it works: I push two bricks simultaneously. The one on the right hand is for me. And the one in my left hand, I pretend it belongs to one of those thumb-sucking bed-wetters in school. Or an imaginary friend. I like imaginary friends better because they can't be held hostage in school by the principal. So I play with them until we don't get along anymore, then I get another one. And when I tire of that, I do something else.

Creating stuff is one of my favorite things to do. I make a fleet of muscle cars and monster trucks with wire hangers and shoe polish tins (for wheels). I do these things because they bring me to a world of imagination. It's also part of self-entertainment, but the real motivation is *cha-ching*! These things fly off the shelves like hot cakes.

Speaking of flying, kites fascinate me. Whenever I fly one, I feel like a pilot. I just let it sail away deep into the blue. And when I'm done, I slowly reel it in for a touchdown. I've taught myself how to make them, and now have a kite biz. I like this biz, too, because it's free to start. Just like my car biz, materials needed to make them are freely available. And making them is as easy as snatching candy from a blind, passed-out baby. All I have to do is gather sticks, plastic bags, wool or yarn, and make them.

Now I am the master kite-maker. I make enough to sell to those booger-eating cootie spreaders while they are getting beat at school. Sometimes I am glad they are at school because they don't have time to learn to do this stuff. And what I like about them is they're willing to spend money on my products. I also take different payments. Some teach me how to write letters and numbers. And others share stories they read in school books for a kite or wire car.

***

Dew: Sounds like 'twas a fair deal to me, too.

Me: Yes, it was. But I was also tryna make 'em see how much fun they could've had, if only they would quit school.

Dew: Sorry you had to push bricks and pretend it was a toy!

Me: Yeah, I know. But those were different times. Nothing like today where kids have so much: Smartphones, Ipads, Xbox, Internet, Social media, TikTok, Five thousand channels on TV, just to name a few.

Sage: I know right! So what did you buy with your hard-earned cash?

Me: I used it on the most important things first: bubblegum and candy and chocolate and other yummy stuff. See, we didn't have an annual candy festival where kids dare people to trick 'em and if they don't want to, they automatically have to treat with candy. So I made mine. After every sale, it was Halloween.

Dew: Yummy! But I also like that you'd trade them for lessons. That was awesome.

Me: Yes, it was. I was a king. And kings hire tutors for private lessons. On a serious note, though, I was feeling left out when they knew how to write their names and I didn't.

Sage: Cool. What other projects did you do?

Me: I had my hands in everything. I'd redesign my clothes - rip them apart, resize them, and then sew them back together. Sometimes I'd just remove sleeves from shirts altogether and wear them sleeveless like cool movie stars. I'd become quite a *fashionisto* and my entire wardrobe was made over.

Dew: Cool. You spent a lot of time alone, exploring your mind. Did any of your exploration ever land you in trouble?

Me: Of course! The next story is about how one day my idle mind got me and my 6 year-old *wifie,* Mae, in trouble. But before I tell y'all, here's a little gem to introduce you to our relationship.

4 mae, my 6-year-old wifie

helluva bivorce

Me and Mae are like two peas in a pod. We spend time together every single day. The only time we are not together is when she's at school, and at night when she's at her house. But on weekends, only sleep separates us. The other two people I see spending so much quality time together are my grandparents. At first I thought they were twins, but my mother says they're not, but married. Now I know when a man spends time with a woman like that, it means they're married. I spend time with Mae, but we're not twins, then it means we're husband and wife. We must be married.

But there's a big problem with our marriage. Unlike my grandparents, we don't sleep in the same house. Every sunset, Mae goes home and returns the next day. I don't know why she is doing this. This is confusing. I need some answers, and who's the best person to ask other than my preteen brother, Si? The guy is only three years older, but he knows everything I know. And more. He has answers to all of my life's questions. So, let's get some answers.

"Si, why doesn't Mae sleep in the same house with me if I'm her husband?"

"Why are you saying you're her husband?"

"Because we spend time together. That means we're married."

"Okay, well, that's because you're getting a divorce," he says.

"What is a bivorce?"

"Divorce, not bivorce. It's when your wife sleeps somewhere else, then one day she comes back and takes your house, your money and your clothes."

"My clothes? She can't take my clothes. Girls don't wear boys' clothes."

"She won't, but her husband will."

"You're saying she's gonna take my clothes and let me wear them? What's the problem then?"

"Not you, her new husband!"

"She has another one? How do you know all this?"

"Because I'm older than you. Now gimme your money. I'll keep it safe for you so she doesn't take it."

"No! I'm going to bury it behind the house so she won't find it. Wait, how will she carry the house? It's too big."

"She won't have to because she's gonna kick you out."

"But I won't leave."

"Well, the police will force you to leave."

"I don't like this bivorce of yours. It stinks."

After our exchange, I'm ready to confront Mae. So, as soon as she drops by, I waste no time.

"Mae, we have to talk. Are we getting a bivorce?"

"What is a bivorce?"

"I don't know, but my brother says you're going to take my clothes and stuff?"

"I don't wear boys' clothes."

"That's what I told him, but he said you're going to give them to your new husband."

"*Ew,* I don't have a new husband."

"I knew he was lying. Okay, you can have my five pennies if you want it. Let's dig it out of the ground."

"Why is the money buried underground?"

"I was hiding it. My brother said you'd take it away from me."

***

Dew: Aww, y'all were so cute! And your brother...

Me: Yeah, he knew everything. He was the *google* to all of my life's questions. But he also messed with my mind all the time. He even introduced me to a word I'd never heard of before. I guess this was the best description from a 10-year-old. It was like someone had been through a helluva bivorce.

Sage: Right, let's move on. What's next?

Me: A lifetime adventure!

5 an afternoon in the belly of earth

"We are down here. Please, hellllp!" This is a part of my life where my sense of adventure fails me... and my Mae.

It's 1979, and I am about to send my family and the village *peoples* on a scary manhunt for an entire day. My day starts as usual—I'm with my grandparents at home while kids are at school. But to my surprise, I see Mae coming to my house. Guess she didn't go to school today.

After playing in the house, we venture outdoors. Today I have in mind something we haven't done before: a picnic in the earth's belly.

"If we're going to have a picnic, don't we need food and soda?" Mae asks.

"Don't worry, Mae, I know just the right place to pay a little visit."

I have my great uncle and aunt's food pantry on my mind. They always have their cabinets overflowing with extra goodies. And they live next door.

"Follow me. It's time to get some groceries."

We walk through the cornfield so nobody sees us. When we get there, no one is home. My "grocery store" is left unattended. I peep through the window to make sure no one is inside, sleeping. "Great uncle, are you in there, sleeping?"

[No answer]

I knock on the kitchen door. Still no one answers. "Okay, Mae, the coast is clear. We can go inside now."

I open the door and lead Mae into the *goodies* heaven and start "grocery shopping" immediately. After filling a pillowcase, we drag it to our picnic hideout: a half-dug toilet pit at the back of their cornfield. Some lazy diggers quit before finishing the job.

When we get there, we send our supplies down in a single drop. Next, it's our bodies. We don't stop and discuss who should jump in first. But if we had, it might have gone something like this: *"Okay Mae, ladies first. Go for it, chap chap!"*

"No, you first. You're the man."

And that assertion of man-hood would've just done it.

Anyway, to impress my girl, I jump in first and sadly land smack on my buttocks. *Ouch!* Things we do to impress HER. I look up and give her the green light. She takes her plunge and crashes onto me. “Hey, watch what you’re doing! That hurts,” I cry, but Mae says nothing.

So far, everything is going as planned. We are now a few feet down underground and ready to start the picnic. We begin our adventure by gobbling up and gulping down our *stolen* goodies.

After feasting, we play “mommy and daddy” with Mae’s dolls. But suddenly she has a change of heart. “I don’t want to be here anymore. I wanna get out!” she cries.

Until now, we weren’t aware that we were stuck underground. See, dropping in was easy. All we had to do was close our eyes, and go “yippee” as we plunged. But getting out is another story. Mae tries to climb out, but she can’t. The ditch is too wide. There’s nowhere to hold on. There are strings of roots that were exposed by the digging, but are not strong enough to support her weight.

After a few unsuccessful attempts, she gets frustrated and stops. Reality kicks in for both of us: we’re trapped in a toilet pit. Mae can’t hold it in anymore. She breaks down and weeps hysterically. ”I wanna go home! Get me out of here. I don’t wanna die here!”

“You’re not gonna die here, Mae. I’ll get you out, okay!” I try to calm her down, but she prefers screaming like a scared little girl. So I let her suit herself. “Okay, you can cry as much as you want, but don’t flood this pit with tears and drown us!”

Mae is a real crybaby, so she wails nonstop. But now I can't take it anymore. *Shush, shush*! Still she won’t shush, so I plug my ears with my fingers to keep out her annoying, whining voice. Mae weeps until she’s tired of it. Now her eyes have run out of tears. There’s no more sound coming out of her mouth.

After all that unnecessary hard work, she falls. Twice. First, on the ground like a bag of potatoes. Second, *asleep* like a nursing baby. Mae is a thumb sucker, so I ensure her silence by forcing her thumb into her mouth. “Hey, open up. Here, sucky-sucky,” she complies and snores away.

But with this loud mouth in Lala-Land, it is too quiet. It’s like I switched the “scream radio” off. Now I feel all alone. Scared. So I wake her up so she can keep crying. Her cry is annoying, but is better than the terrifying silence. Mae cries louder than before. But that scares me. So I join her.

With both of us hollering, it’s like we are in a crying contest. When she looks at me crying, she gets more terrified and sobs even louder. I do likewise. Occasionally, we try comforting one another, but that doesn’t help. The contest continues until I don’t hear our sound anymore.

About an hour later, I wake up to voices. It's the village people searching for us. Someone (probably the smartest person on the planet) thought of checking the ditch. “Hellllp! We are down here!” I scream at the top of my lungs. "Mae, Mae, wake up!” I say, tapping her on her forehead. “We are down here. Please, get us out of here!” Mae wakes up but continues crying. “Hey, stop crying. We are getting out of here. They’ve found us!” I hear more voices."Hellllp!" As they get closer, I hear my uncle’s voice.

“Okay kids, we are gonna get you out of there. Just stay put!” He quickly lowers a step ladder. I tell Mae I have to get out first in case the ladder breaks after one use. Mae doesn’t agree with me. So I let her go first just because she won’t stop bawling. A few steps up, Mae stops.

“Why are you stopping, Mae?”

“Because I am scared I am going to fall.”

“You will not fall. Okay, I'll help you out. Put your buttocks on my head, but don’t fart on me, okay?”

"It's okay Mae, come up. You won't fall," uncle says. That does it for Mae. She takes a few more steps and out she goes. I get on the ladder and make my way out, too. We walk to an open space in front of my house. When we get there, the entire community is gathering. People shouting gibberish things, others are crying. I can’t tell if they’re shedding tears of joy and relief, or frustration and anger, but whatever it is, it is too darn loud and confusing.

In the middle of all that confusion, someone sneaks in a skin-ripping pinch on me. “You kids are naughty! What were you doing in that hole? You had all of us worried the entire afternoon,” she says as she pinches my earlobe with her seventy-something old vice-grip-like dead nails. “And what were you going to do with those eggs we found next to the hole?”

“We were going to fry them in the hole but we forgot them outside,” Mae says.

I try to shush her, but she doesn’t listen to me. She tells everything.

Finally, the dead nails release me. But little do I know that this nip is just an intro. The plan to “teach us a lesson” is underway. People are gathered at the *kangaroo(f)* court waiting for us, and the sticks are being picked up by someone. Yes, we are in trouble.

But I can’t understand what kind of people these are. Do they even understand how much emotional trauma we’ve already suffered? I guess not because someone just tried to rip off my ear lobes. This is too much to handle. I gotta figure out how to get myself out of this before the sticks arrive.

I scan the *kangaroo(f)* court's perimeter for an escape route. I have to save my buttocks. And mine only. It's every man for himself. And every chic for herself. I am not going down for anyone. Not even for my lady. Nope, not today.

Okay, before you even think of judging me, I want you to understand one thing: Mae is not a sprinter. Think of her like this: in a hundred meter dash with a tortoise, a snail, a sloth, and a starfish, Mae would tie with the sloth for the last place. So with that slowness, they'd catch us before we even started fleeing. I can't risk being caught because of a sluggard. So I'm not taking her on *my* escape mission.

In fact, we're in this mess because of her. If she'd used her head and said "No, I don't think we should have a picnic in a toilet pit. How are we going to get out?", we wouldn't be here. If she had not skipped school today, I wouldn't have raided the pantry and had a picnic. I wouldn't have found myself in deep doo-doo. Okay, there you have it. It's her fault, and she has to take one for the team. Alone. At least that way, only one of us gets spanked. Wouldn't you agree?

Either way, leaving her behind is the smartest thing to do for the team. And if there's a next time, I'll take one for the team as she *strolls* away. But not today!

With my decision made, I look for an opening. Darn it! Security is tight. We are seated on the ground, surrounded by fuming adults deciding our fate. And with the looks on their faces, it's not good.

I see an opening next to *Koko*. This is something I have to take advantage of. So I walk to her and pretend to be wanting something. While she's talking to someone to her left, I squeeze through the tiny space to her right and make a run for my life.

Unfortunately, someone who has nothing better to do with his life but chase kids, comes after me. I speed up, but no matter how hard I push myself, I can't outrun this *loser*. Within seconds, he apprehends me and carries me back to the court. The law enforcers are now angrier. They hand out our sentences. There will be countless lashes on our behinds.

These courts are always unfair to children. Once a kid is accused of a crime, that's it. No negotiations. So, as expected, we don't get a fair trial. None of the jurors bother to give us a chance to present our case. I have no doubt, if given a chance, I could have my penalty reduced. I'd give the speech of my life and put everything on Mae. It's that simple!

6 speech to save my butt, and mine only

dear angry village peoples

Ladies and gentlemen - angry lawmakers and enforcers, before we get a little excited and ahead of ourselves, I'd like to plead "NOT GUILTY." Thank you very much!

See, my accomplice here orchestrated the whole thing. As you all know (or might be aware), she skipped school today just to lure me into this PREMEDITATED crime. I'm a victim here. A vulnerable accomplice (not by choice). She tricked me into accompanying her.

We all know what happened in the Garden of Eden. And we can't forget what happened to the strength and the Jheri Curls of the muscleman, Samson. And just like those giants, I had no chance, either, against her deceitful tongue. So you know, I tried, but I couldn't resist the natural superpowers she possesses as a female species of humankind. Without an inch of doubt, she manipulated me like her *sistrens*, Delilah and Eve, deceived their men.

I hope you recognize that executing such a well thought out scheme, given its intricate nature, requires a knowledgeable, school trained mind. And I hope the jury and everyone here knows that my exploiter is a scholar. She spends five hours each day learning millions of sophisticated tricks in school.

But me, I'm still a little boy - not even potty trained yet. I'm not even in creche (daycare) yet. I can't even write my name, let alone come up with such a sophisticated, well-thought out, complex plot.

I also know that all of you know girls mature much faster than boys. And that advantage, angry adults, gave her an edge in manipulating me. I was just an accomplice who was taken advantage of by a professional exploiter.

I hope everyone can see through it. Only a matured scholar could pull it through. Not an amateur!

So, dear angry village *peoples*, I'd like for you to consider my circumstances here before you lay your sentences. I had nothing to do with the planning or the execution of the crimes we are accused of. She kept all the highly classified information in her calculating mind from me as her subordinate. Thank you for your understanding. I rest my case now.

Oh, one more thing: I'd like to let the jury know that I'm ready to cut a side deal for future crimes she might lure me into.

I fear for my safety in the future. So I think we should sign a cooperation pact right now. That way, I can go undercover right away. I believe together we can foil all of her future plots before she entices and lures me in again. If we do so, I promise to be a reliable informer - the world's number one snitch.

Anytime I find myself unable to resist her persuasive mind, I'll say to myself, "remember the pact you signed with the angry adults? Then I'll answer myself, "Yes, I do." Then I'll say, "Okay, resist and snitch."

I solemnly promise the kangaroo (f) court. Please spare my buttocks today. And thank you in advance for taking your precious time and seeing through the plot of this conniving, self-serving mastermind.

I rest my case... for the last time this time. Thank you and remember, I'm on your side here."

Now, with that pleading, I think they'd have let me off with a warning. Unfortunately, it was just a dream. The *meanies* had decided, so they whipped us as planned. After that, I vowed to take no one on my ventures again. Not even *Bae*.

***

Dew: [All worked up] I cannot believe what you've just said about Mae... just to save yourself? What about her?

Me: Okay, Dew, I can understand the "sisterhood of traveling pants" feelings, but I think you missed the point here. I didn't actually give the speech.

Sage: M46, I'd have done the same.

[Dew turns her attention to Sage]

Dew: Sage!? I can't believe you, either. I see what's going on here. You're just saying it because you're a boy.

Sage: Don't be ridiculous, Dew. I'm not. I'm just saying it because I hate spankings.

Dew: But what about empathy? Caring for others? Why not save her skin, too? She's human, too, you know!

Sage: I know that. But, me too, I'd have left her behind. The girl couldn't even beat a snail in a hundred meter dash.

Me: Hey guys, no need to be at each other's throats. Sage, Dew is right. But Dew, don't forget, this is a comedy book.

Dew: Comedy book, or not, I take it seriously.

Me: Okay, I get where you're coming from. In fact, I have an idea. Y'all should debate this "sexism" thing in the classroom with your teacher as a peacemaker.

Dew: Oh yeah, we're definitely doing that. Actually, I have a better idea. You should be there, too, because you started it!

Me: Just name the place, the time, the date, and I'll be there.

Dew: I'll let you know after I talk to Ms. Bretsch. And you Sage, why are you quiet now? You're scared. Is it because you know the girls are gonna win?

Sage: Ain't scared. Bring it on. Wait, what's the debate gonna be about?

Dew: Your sexist comments. And you can't take it back.

Sage: But that wasn't sexist. I only said I'd have saved my skin.

Dew: You're responding to a sexist statement, made by a sexist, so you're a sexist!

Me: Dew, that's an intense statement, don't you think?

Dew: No, I don't think so!

Me: You know, I have three daughters. Being sexist is the last thing—

Dew: Three daughters or not, leaving your girl behind was being sexist, immature, cold, inhumane, outright wrong, and honestly, troubling. I need a break.

[Dew gets up and walks away]

Me: Wow, this girl is on fire. I think we need to pray for peace right now before she starts World War III, Sage.

Sage: It's because of you, M46. You got us in trouble with the "Me Too" people.

Me: Are you blaming me? It was your fault, you shouldn't have said, "I'd have done the same"

Sage: How was I supposed to know? You can't blame me!

[Dew returns]

Dew: Why are y'all whispering?

Me: Yeah boy, speak up. What's the matter with you, sonny boy? Lost your voice... or your mind?

Dew: I am sorry I got all worked out there. It's just that I take this stuff seriously.

Me: I am glad you stand up for what you believe in.

Dew: Thank you. Please, tell us more about your childhood.

7 queen II king

rats, the masters of devouring

The tragedy of my childhood is that my mother has to choose between raising me and raising someone else's children. "This is a tough choice," she tells me. So as a single mom, who has to care for her five other children and her parents, she doesn't choose in my favor.

Right after my second birthday, she takes a live-in housekeeping job in the city, leaving me under the care of her parents. My grandparents are fun and everything, and I love being with them, but I'd rather be with my mother. I still need to be nursed by her. I still need to be babied. Unfortunately, that's just a dream. Her job has taken her away from me. And I hate it. Sometimes I feel unloved or forgotten.

Mother is always gone for months (sometimes up to six) before returning. And when she finally does, it's usually for a two-day weekend visit. But that is not enough time to make up for months of absence. If anything, it is just a tease. Even worse, I never know when Mother is coming back. There is no set schedule. There are no telephones. She doesn't write. So we don't talk.

But on the nights that she comes back, Mr. NT, the local shuttle driver, drops her off around midnight. She comes in and immediately catches up with her parents for hours. That's their thing. But I have my thing too: I stay asleep until I hear her voice. Then I jump out of the bed like a soldier on discharge day and run to the living room.

***

It's Saturday around 9 p.m. I'm in *Koko*'s bed. But I am not asleep. Why am I in my grandma's bed? This is what I do. I sleep with her because she's my mother when my other mother isn't here. I also sleep with her so she can nurse me. But I always wake up *hangry* with a stomach full of air. *Koko* tells me that's because she's seventy years old. I don't know what that means, but I don't ask her.

I keep my fingers crossed Mother comes back tonight. I do this every weekend, waiting with great anticipation. So every time I hear the sound of a car outside, I dash to the window and peep. I've been fighting sleep, waiting to hear her voice for hours. But now I can't fight anymore. So I fall asleep. About two hours later, I come out of a dream. I don't remember much about it. But I think Mother was in it. I turn and feel for *Koko*. She's not in bed. There's only one place she can be: the living room. I listen carefully. Soft voices travel into my ears. I feel the excitement, but I restrain myself. I have been disappointed before.

The voices continue. Seconds later, I hear the pleasant voice I've been waiting for. It is my mother's, the one that is always gone. I hop out of the bed, throw *Koko's* blankets on the floor and race to the living room. At first, I can't see Mother in the flickering candlelight. Then I see her sitting on the floor. I see *Koko* and my other siblings, too. I just give them "the look" which means, you all knew Mother was back, but you didn't wake me up. I am not your friend anymore.

I run to my mommy and throw myself on her lap. After a few seconds of catching up, I ditch her and stick my fingers in her bags. She reaches in one parcel and pulls out some goodies. My eyes light up. It's everything I imagined: lollipops, Licorice All sorts candy, chocolate bars, biscuits [cookies]. Also contained in the bag are breads of all kinds. But they're not on the top of my list, so I don't touch them.

For now, I stuff my mouth with sweets. I gag, but that doesn't stop me. I devour and finish everything. See, I've learned that important lesson from our uninvited guests: rats. Rats are the masters of devouring. They eat and finish everything at one go because they know the secret: tomorrow isn't promised. So, like my little friends, I lick even the tiniest crumbs on the floor.

See, as the youngest sibling, you must learn tricks, because the older siblings play tricks on you and eat your stuff.

***

Once the goodies fest is over, it's time to go back to bed. But for me, it's also time to wash down everything. Mother suggests I go back to *Koko's* bed. This is unusual. Something is unpleasantly strange. And I don't like it. Not a bit. So I protest. "But I always sleep with you when you're home because I don't get to see you much, mommy."

—the betrayal

Mother agrees but tells me I can't sleep with her because she's brought a friend. I am not amused. See, Mother normally comes back alone, and I'm used to that. But now she's telling me there's someone else in the house and she's ditching me for a complete stranger. I don't appreciate it.

Okay, honestly, I don't really mind visitors, but this business of bringing enemies into my house in the middle of the night is not cool. What's also not cool is dropping news on me at the last minute. I mean, there's a foe in mommy's bed, and I haven't been told about it until now. This is a big problem. Totally unacceptable. I've been betrayed!

Okay, one minute I was feasting and bouncing off the walls, and the next I'm competing for my spot on the bed. This is messed up. And the worst part is I am losing and I can't do anything about it. At least for now. I really don't understand what happened to my mother - the sudden change of behavior. Who is this person? What has she done with my mother? An outsider has come between us and turned her against me. And I can't convince her otherwise.

This is a crisis. Things are changing between us. Our bonding custom is in danger of being changed because of a stranger. It's clear Mother has been turned into a sellout. And as for *Koko,* she is guilty for not teaching her daughter good manners — not to ever diss me like this. In fact, everyone in this house is guilty of something... anything that has to do with this. The fact that people are willing to change a long-held family tradition without seeking my counsel is a serious crime. Up there with treason.

This is not how things should go down in a normal society. You can't just change a family tradition for a stranger. An enemy!

***

I'm not impressed with Mother's move, so I launch my best verbal resistance. "Mother, I have to sleep with you. The stranger can sleep outside on the porch with the dog. It's not raining."

My words fall on deaf ears. But I have a fragile birthright to protect. And I am determined to do whatever it takes. With no chance of changing minds, I move to the only option available: turn a queen into a king.

One by one, I drag three dining room chairs to the bedroom and carefully align them next to the bed. Next, I fit the chair bases with two soft, giant, goose down pillows for the cushy pillow top experience. Once my makeshift California King-size bed is all set, I slide in and make myself comfy. I pull her bed covers over me and reach for *nyanya* [sucky-sucky]. Once secured in my mouth, I begin sucking until I fall into a deep, peaceful slumber.

—the trauma

Seven hours later, I wake up in terror. I'm all alone, laying in the middle of the *queen* with a tummy full of air. My *king* is gone — the chairs are not where I'd put them. And there's a dummy [pacifier] in my mouth. First, I joyfully suck on it. Then, it hits me. Something is not right. This is not what I had in my mouth when I went to sleep. I slept on real *nyanya*, not this stupid rubber. And Mother is missing. The enemy, too. But I don't mind that one missing. It's my mother I'm worried about. My eyes pop wide open. I remember the other times when I fell victim to the same thing. So I jump out of bed, take a few steps, turn back around and throw the blankets on the ground. I am mad!

Then I search around the house. She's nowhere to be found. I can't hear her voice, either. The house is totally quiet. I go from room to room, turning the entire house upside down. Still no sign of her. After searching everywhere, my worst nightmare is confirmed. Mother is gone. She's left me. AGAIN.

I yank the "dummy" out of my mouth and throw it away and begin screaming. Everyone else is still asleep, but I don't care about waking them up. They're all just as "cruel" because they let me sleep while Mother snuck out and left me. The way I see it, everyone is guilty of treachery. And because they did nothing to stop her, or at least wake me up, none of them deserve a peaceful early morning sleep. Everyone has to get up.

Case closed! "Mother?! Mother?!" I scream. No answer. "*Koko*? *Koko*? Wake up, she's gone!" I yell even louder.

***

I am a stubborn kid. Once I start crying, I won't stop until it hurts. Even then, I don't completely stop. I go through the pain until *Koko* intervenes again, or I fall asleep. See, in my head I think people expect you to cry and stop, so they don't give you special attention. But I'm vulnerable right now. I need special care.

Also, I can't be seen as someone who starts crying and stops without a reason. That would mean I was crying for no reason in the first place. So I never stop on my own. I can't. Someone has to baby me. But if no one cares that much, then so be it. I weep until I lose my voice first. That way they know I didn't really stop crying. I just didn't have a voice to express it. I can't be seen as giving up.

See, one thing you should know about me is I'm one of those kids who doesn't mind crying for twenty-four hours non- stop. I cry so much that I even do it when I'm eating. What I do is I chew, stop and cry again until tears and saliva and snot mix up on my face. Then I wipe my face with my clothes and continue. Think that's disgusting? Wait until you see me in action!

My eldest brother, Kwaito, always says crying reduces the amount of water in my head. I don't know what he really means by that, but I guess today the inside of my head will be dry as a desert.

***

It's been three days since she left. And the new cycle has officially begun. I wake up crying hysterically. Then I search every room. I don't really know why, but I think I do it in case we're playing *Hide and Seek* and I wasn't told.

With no sign of Mother in the house, I wait and cry at the gate. I guess I'm hoping each day will be the day she comes back. I wait and wait and wait. Then grandma *(Koko)* puts me on her back and wraps me with a blanket.

I fall asleep. Then I have a nightmare of Mother leaving me. I wake up and pick up from where I left off. *Koko* ends the piggy back ride because I'm screaming in her ears. I head back to the gate, where I cry until dusk. Sometimes I tire of crying and waiting, but I'm trapped by stubbornness. So I carry on. I give myself breaks from crying by talking to myself as if I were talking to Mother.

"You're coming back mommy, okay?"

"Yes, I'm coming back, baby."

"Okay mommy, but I'll wait for you here, okay!"

I have these little chit chats to calm myself down. I do it for hours, switching between the crying and the "pretend-she's-here" self-talk. But as soon as the thought of not seeing her crosses my mind, the talk is over. It's time for some serious business. I bawl until another intervention.

***

Sage: *[Teasing]* Did the inside of your head become dry like a desert?

Dew: Sage, that's not nice. I'm sorry, Mrm46.

Me: Hey, don't y'all get all *emo* on me now.

Dew: But that was really sad. But why did your mom only stay for one night, not the entire weekend?

Me: *Koko* told me later that she was on one of her rare days off and came home for a few hours.

Dew: Aww, sorry, Mrm46! Okay, let's move on. What's next?

8 a frightened boy: the negotiations

charge # 4: refusal to transport a plaintiff

Did you know we are born with only two kinds of fear? You and *me* and everyone else were born with a fear of *loud sounds* and fear of *falling*. Everything else we learn through scary encounters as we grow. For me, thanks to my brother, Si, that list grew two-fold before I could learn to write my name.

Living with my grandparents in the countryside is cool and everything, *but* what's not cool is, we don't have an indoor bathroom *or* electricity. And not having those "luxuries" is a problem for me, especially at night.

Our iron sheet toilet is installed a hundred-fifty feet away from the house. Okay, between you and me, I think putting the small house that far was outright stupid. Why would anyone do that when there's so much free space in front of our house? We literally have enough space to have a hundred of those erected there. This is totally unacceptable. So, I have a little chit chat with the patriarch of the family.

"Err... Grandpa, there's something that's been on my chest for some time now. So I think we should talk. Man to man." Okay, it didn't actually go like that. I cut straight to the chase. "Why is our toilet in another village, Grandpa?

Grandpa chuckles as he puts me on his lap. "Because it's a pit toilet, grandson," he says. "It has to be that far away from the house so we don't get sick."

Did he just say, "so we don't get sick?" Or am I hearing things? Please don't tell me *he expects me to be convinced by that lame excuse?* Because I am not. Anyway, as a reasonable guy, I get it. He doesn't want a pit toilet indoors. But he should've placed it four feet away from the front door. That way, when nature calls, it would be a spit throw away, so I can just jump from our door, and *Voila!* I'm in. Take care of my biz and leap back into the house in two seconds. Three, tops.

If he's not comfortable with that, he can add a foot. I'll even settle for six; nothing more. But don't gimme the "so we don't get sick" excuse. I don't care about getting sick. I just want numbers - five or six feet; two or three seconds.

"Okay, Grandpa, nobody gets sick from smelling *poo-pee.* If anything, we might get a little woozy-dizzy. Please, move it closer."

Grandpa is hard-headed. Before I can even tell him "poo-pee" means poop and pee together, he objects. So I follow up with a one-man, one-signature petition to pressure him to change his mind.

"Grandpa, I've got enough signatures on this petition so you have to move the toilet."

Still, he doesn't honor my wishes. Okay, that's it! Being nice isn't getting my point across. So I take off my nice-guy mask and go back to the negotiation table with a threat. "That's it, old man. If you don't move it, I'm taking you to the *kangaroo*(f) court."

See, the idea is to scare him, but to my shock, Grandpa welcomes my threat with open arms. He even shares a secret. "I am going to tell everyone we've been digging our toilets there long before you were born."

You see what he's doing, right? Okay, I admit, he's right. The poop houses were dug there before I was even born. And he has every right to put it wherever he pleases, after all, it's his poop house; his property. But this isn't over yet. I'm just getting started. "Well, that's true Grandpa, but once I was here - potty trained and everything- you should have moved it closer," I fire back.

Grandpa still disagrees. *Argh, stubborn old man.* It's time for the *kangaroo (f)* court to solve this matter once and for all. But first, I have to build a strong legal team. To do so, I visit my grand-uncle, his little brother, who lives next door. I tell him my problem with his older brother. He gets up and pours two cups of tea and offers me one. "You will not win against *abuti* [brother]," he warns.

"I don't drink hot tea in the heat, great-uncle. Please, let's stay focused. And why are you saying I'm not gonna win?"

The great one takes a sip, slightly burning the tip of his tongue and says, "because your grandfather is one of the respected elders in the community. So he'll be the one presiding over the case. And he's going to rule in his favor because he's right."

"But that's not fair." I get up and throw a tantrum.

He follows up with old people's favorite thing to say, "Yes, great-nephew, life is not always fair."

Now I am really disappointed with him. He chose his brother's side over mine. So I head back to tell grandpa I won't be taking him to court after all. I share what his brother said would happen if I did. I also tell him it's not fair. He counters with a speech about life not being fair... and how to learn to live with it. Blah. Blah. Blah.

While he's blah blah-ing away, I get another idea. "Grandpa, can you take me to the next village so I can have their *kangaroo (f)* court hear my case?

I'm confident that he wouldn't be deciding the cases there. Another shocker! Instead of honoring my request, he informs me that the villages work together, so he'll be judging there, too. But somehow, I'm not crushed this time around. I feel like he's just given me more incriminating info to build an even stronger case: Charge # 1- *Refusing to move the toilet closer.* Charge # 2- *Unfairness - nobody should judge their own criminal case.* And Charge # 3 - *Deciding cases in over one village.*

Now, with all these charges, I think I got him. I'm confident I'll win. That's if he takes me. "Grandpa, can you take me now? I don't have all day!" Still, he refuses to. So I add another charge: *refusal to transport a plaintiff.*

I head back to my great-uncle and ask him to take me, but he refuses as well. I'm really disappointed with these old men. Because I don't know where the next village is, and the one after, I have to let it go. Grandpa wins. I lose. But I still believe that putting the toilet in front of the house is a genius idea. And not doing so is stupid.

—when nature calls at night

The worst time for nature to call is after nightfall, especially when you live in a village where toilets stand hundreds of feet away from houses. And there's no electricity. Those two things make living on the farm unpleasant for me.

Truth is, the distance itself – though never fun when the stomach is running – is not much of an issue during the day. But after nightfall, everything changes. Suddenly, it matters. Fifty yards feels like a hundred yards. And the toilet disappears from your sight, like someone steals it and returns it each morning.

Anyway, there are these solutions that everyone uses: grandparents keeping night potties to save themselves the trips. And everyone else uses candles, flashlights, or lanterns to find their way, But this doesn't work for me. Not at this age. See, when I was a baby I had it made. I just soiled the napkins (diapers) and let my mother worry about cleaning the mess. Just a *"Waaa"* took away all my poop problems. But now my glory days are gone. I am too old for a napkin; too young for a senior citizens' potty.

My only option is to rely on light like everyone who is not a senior citizen yet. But I have a problem with that. Especially candle light. See, when it's raining or windy, candles are the worst. The flame gets distinguished, leaving you in harm's way. And that's exactly what happened to me on my very first attempt. And trust me, it's not a great experience!

9 an offer *he* can't refuse

It's a windy August evening when I receive a sudden call.

Brrring! Brrring! "Hello?"

"Oh hi, this is nature calling. You have to go use it now!"

"But it's dark outside."

"I don't care! Now, go!"

"Okay, coming. But first I have to find a companion."

I've heard horror stories about how so-and-so got lost after losing their lights on their way to the toilet. So I am too scared to face the dark alone. "Si, I need to go. Can you walk me to the toilet?" My words fall on deaf ears.

Okay, let's back-peddle for a sec here and talk about this brother-o-mine. First off, this guy has never been a hero in his brief life, and here I am giving him an opportunity. A chance to shine and prove himself to be useful. But what does he do?

Refuses an offer he shouldn't. I don't get it. Why would anyone turn down a once-in-a-lifetime gift like this?

Still, as a thoughtful guy, I don't get all worked up and lose my cool. I give him another chance. "Pretty please, can you walk me?"

He ignores me and continues to work out his biceps with a bucket full of water. Okay, now I get it. His little muscles are more important than me having an accident on myself. But I have a different argument here. Girls at this age don't care about Popeye's big spinach arms - unless you are Olive Oyl. They're into gentle-hearted bravehearts who walk their little brothers to the toilets. And here I am offering him the quickest and surest route to a girl's heart, but he just can't see it.

You know, some people are really blind. An opportunity can be dancing, *macarena* in front of them, and they still wouldn't see it. Clearly, this muscle-man-wanna-be is one of those visually impaired, scared-to-be-hero whippersnappers.

Still, as a nice guy, I don't give up on him. So I beg him to open his eyes and see the value of my offer. He still refuses.

Okay, I know one is not supposed to quit on those who don't know how a girl's heart works. But sometimes you just have to accept it: people don't appreciate a good offer until it's gone. So I give up on him. Reluctantly.

With no one to accompany me, I turn to Topsy. "Topsy? Come here, girl. Can you walk me to the toilet?" No answer. She is not home. I think she is out and about searching for her boyfriend in the neighborhood.

Now I'm in trouble: Either I man up and face my fears, or chicken out and let nature take its course. Okay, option two is a no-no. So I put my shoes on to avoid a messy situation. I grab a candle and give myself a pep talk. "Don't look up no matter what happens!" I have to keep my eyes away from the sky; that's where my biggest enemy is. [I'll get to that later]

Emboldened by my pep talk, I step outside. The night's blanket of darkness engulfs me. I take a deep breath and take my next step. The door slams closed behind me, sending chills down my spine. "I can do this!" I reassure myself.

It's pitch black. All I can see is the precious tiny light from the candle. So I keep my eyes on the ground and carefully tiptoe as quietly as possible. Occasionally, tilting my head up slightly to get a view of the poop house. As I trudge forward, the hundred-fifty-yard distance suddenly feels like eight miles of walking through a ghost town. So I whisper my pep repeatedly.

Murphy's Law states, "Anything that can go wrong will go wrong." About halfway through, I hear a spooky sound. I stop and listen. It's not a human sound. It is like a combination of a howling wind and a hooting owl. The noise ceases. "*Hello! Is someone out there? This is not funny. Hello! I'm not scared of you. I have a candle and I'm not afraid to use it. Show your face, coward, and I'll burn you with this light. C'mon. Come and get me, you fat, ugly monster!*"

Okay, I don't say that. But that's what people always say in scary movies. Why do they do that? Because every time they do, the beast appears, as requested, and... I don't get it; not only does it let the monster know they're scared, but it gives away their location. Don't you think that's dumb? What if the monster is blind?

Anyway, I'm not trying to be that kind of victim. Not gonna let the beasts of the night track me down with my voice.

They'll have to work a little harder for this human flesh. So I keep my mouth shut and plod forward.

—a monster with a sense of humor

Suddenly, the spooky noise returns. This time it's louder. My hair stands on end. My heart beats faster and my body shakes. I slowly rotate my head but about thirty degrees. Then something pops up out of nowhere and races towards me. Super-fast!

"Hellllp!!" I shriek in horror as I tumble to the ground. The candle flies out of my hand. The darkness swallows the flame. Suddenly, I can't see anything anymore. Not the footpath. Not the toilet. Not even our house. All I can see is nothing but darkness. I lay on my stomach motionless as horrific thoughts flood my head. I imagine hideous beasts eating me alive. Then a barrage of questions follows. "What was that? Where did it go? Why didn't it eat me?"

"Wait a minute, something really weird has happened here," I think to myself. The thing, whatever it was, not only knocked me down but also gave me a wedgie in the process. Possibly the fastest wedgie on record. Now I'm confused. What kind of monster does that? This thing isn't your ordinary blood-thirsty-ready-to-destroy-monster. Because whatever it is, it has a *sick* sense of humor.

The more I think of it, the more I doubt it was an actual monster. What kind of monster gives kids wedgies on their way to the poop house? I've never heard of a monster that runs to you, pulls your pants up, and flees. Real monsters are not into pranks. They're out to eat you. And they don't care if you're going to poop, they just eat you and your poop. And maybe later, poop your poop. But never you.

***

When in danger, pangolins roll themselves into balls; turtles retract their head back into their shells; skunks shoot smelly liquids. But I have none of those sophisticated defense mechanisms. So I close my eyes, suck my thumb and lay there stock-still, pretending to be dead.

[Nothing happens]

The weird sounds cease. Now I only hear crickets chirping. I crawl and search for my candle in the weeds, sandwiching the footpath. "Yes!" I celebrate as I pick it up. But something is strange --it is harder, and has dents all around. *Argh,* it's a bare corn cob. I throw it away and keep searching. Still with my eyes closed.

Finally, I feel my candle wedged between the weeds. I do a mental victory dance. But then it hits me. The candle is useless now; the lighter is in the house.

—the return

Without light, I face a new challenge. Do I move forward or do I return? In the midst of my confusion, something incredible happens: nature hangs up. With my troubles behind me, I rise, with my candle drawn like a warrior's dagger. I put a grip on my shorts –just in case the wedgie master returns for another stunt--and search for my way back.

It's so dark; it feels like I am wandering blindfolded through a graveyard. Suddenly, the spooky sound returns. I stop, shut my eyes and wait silently. Once again, the thing scurries towards me and sends me to the ground. This time I clutch on to my candle, but it breaks.

After a few seconds of summoning some courage, I get up and wield it again. With the front piece pointed to the ground.

"Hey, why do you keep on tripping me? Ugly beast! I'm not scared of you. If you do that again, I'm gonna poke your fat belly with this candle," I threaten.

***

Remember when I told you that people are dumb for giving out their locations? I still think so. And yes, I know I just did it. But this is different. Based on my "monster's" actions, he's not a real monster, but a silly monster-wanna-be trying to scare me and amuse himself.

As I continue searching for my way back to the house, I hear another noise. A rather pleasant one. It's my doggy. Topsy continues to bark from a distance. I think she does not know who I am.

I listen carefully and let the sound guide me as I race towards it. The closer I get, the more she barks. Finally, she recognizes me and runs to give me one of those military-style homecoming welcomes. And with her guidance, I make it back to the house safely.

***

"Why did you gimme a wedgie?" I immediately confront my brother.

"It wasn't me."

"Yes, it was because monsters don't give kids wedgies."

"I don't know what you're talking about."

"Yes, you do."

This guy is good at denying things. Whenever you accuse him of something, he can deny it until you start thinking you're crazy.

***

Dew: Aw, Mrm46, I'm sorry he did that to you. Did he ever come clean?

Me: Yeah, but years later.

Dew: Lol, at least he did. Okay, tell us the story about the man on the moon.

Me: Sure.

—the man on the moon

Without electricity, we rely on an open fire for everything. We make it to boil water for bathing and making tea. At night, we use it to cook our meals. We even use it to keep our bodies warm during winter nights.

Evening fires are my favorite. We gather around and listen to grandpa's stories. The stories are always magical. Even the sad and scary ones. This is a special time for me because I love the entertainment, but for my brother, it's not the stories that excite him.

When story-time is over, and my grandparents go inside, it's time for his shenanigans. He grabs the limelight and performs his magic tricks on me.

"Do you see that man on the moon staring at you?" he asks, pointing at the moon.

[After examining it for a few seconds, I do see a shape resembling his claim]

"Yes. But what is he doing, sitting on the moon?"I ask.

"He's watching you."

"Why is he watching me?"

"Because he's a cannibal. He catches kids who stay out late and eat them up."

"But he can't catch me. I'm gonna kick him like a soccer ball."

[Pause]

"Wait, why does he wanna eat me, not his vegetables?"

"He's a cannibal. He only eats kids. Do you see the fork in his hand?"

[I take another good look, and see the shape of a fork]

"Yes, I see it. But what is it for?"

"He uses it to eat kids. If you don't run to the house now, he's gonna eat you."

"But how will he *braai* [barbecue] me? He doesn't have fire."

"He doesn't need fire. His fork is made of flames."

Okay, my brother's threats are getting to me. Maybe it would be wise to negotiate with the hungry man.

"Mr. Cannonball, you can eat my corn. But don't eat me, okay! Do you hear me, Mr. Cannonball?"

"He's a cannibal, not a cannonball."

"Okay. Do you hear me, Mr. Carnival?"

[No answer]

"Why is he not answering me?"

"Because you keep giving him names."

"I'm not. You're the one who called him cannonball and when I call him that, you say he's, carnival."

"Shhh! Did you see that?"

"See what? What happened?"

"Didn't you see him move? He's coming for you."

[I look up, and he's no longer there. The clouds are moving across the moon]

“Noooo, don’t come get me, Mr. Carnival! I don’t want you to eat me up!”

“If you don’t want him to eat you, run to the house. Now!

“But what about my corn?”

“You told him he can have it.”

“Okay, but tell him if he wants to go to heaven, he must stop eating people’s corn,” I shout as I sprint to the house.

***

Dew: Aww!

Me: Poor little me. I’d fallen for it.

***

About half an hour later, my brother comes in. I get out of my hideout.

“Did he come? Did he eat my corn?”

“All of it,” he says, handing me a naked cob.

“So he doesn’t wanna go to heaven?”

[I peep through the window and hand Mr. Carnival his judgment]

“Mr. Carnival, you’re going to hell.”

“*Shh*!, stop screaming. You’ll make him come inside,” Si says.

[I don’t pay him attention]

“Satan Lucifer is going to burn you and eat you up. Thief!”

[Once I’m done with the corn thief, I go to the bedroom]

"*Koko*, wake up. Mr. Carnival ate my corn!"

Koko doesn't wake up, but mumbles something. Grandpa is snoring from his bed. Whenever he snores like this, it means he drank his traditional beer, and doesn't wake up for anything. So I crawl under the bed and sit quietly in the dark. I think about everything my brother told me about Mr. Carnival - his flame fork, how he wants to eat me, and how he magically disappeared from the sky.

I can't sleep because I'm afraid he'll eat me in my sleep. So I tiptoe to the kitchen and barricade the door with chairs. I do the same in the living room. Once they're jammed shut, I go back to the room and lie down with one eye slightly open, listening for any suspicious sounds. I stand guard as long as I can.

In the morning, I emerge from under the bed and race to the living room like it's Christmas day. Only I'm checking if the corn thief came. He didn't. Do you know how I know? First, I'm not in his fat belly and, second, the chairs are still pushed up underneath the doorknobs.

Mr. Carnival doesn't sit on the moon when it's raining. I think he's afraid of lightning. So those nights are a special treat. I know for sure he won't be up there. And just to show him who's boss [in case he's invisible], I run outside and stick my tongue out and spit at him. Sometimes the spit comes back and falls on my face, but it doesn't matter because it's my night, not his.

But now I'm tired of fleeing to the house while my brother enjoys himself outside. I wanna stay, too, but not have him eat me. So I come up with a plan. Tonight I'll bring chili powder to the fire and burn him if he tries to eat me.

—the plan to burn Mr. Carnival's mouth

"Storytime is over. You should go to the house!" Simon says.

"No, I want to teach Mr. Carnival a lesson," I tell him as I remove a box from my pocket.

"What are you talking about? And what are you doing with chili pepper?"

"It's for Mr. Carnival. Mr. Carniv-a-a-a-a-l, come and get me. I'm gonna burn your mouth if you try to eat me," I yell, mixing the chili powder with saliva. When the paste is ready, I rub it all over my body and head. *Argh!* I have forgotten about the open sores and dandruff on my head. "Help me, I am burning up!" I came to burn Mr. Carnival, but now I'm the one on fire.

Instead of helping me, Si burst out laughing. There's no time to ask him again, so I dash to the house to wash off the chili. Darn it! The water container is empty. There's only one place full of cold water right now, and it's about a hundred feet away. So I turn around and race past my brother.

"Hey, where are you running to?" he yells.

"I'm going to jump into the well! There's no water in the house!"

Si gets up and chases after me. Usually older brothers catch up with you in no time, but he can't. I'm flying. When I get there, I toss off the lid and throw my head in first. But something unpleasant is happening: I can't move beyond the mouth of the well. My shoulders refuse to move out of the way.

I am stuck. Head in; body out. And I'm burning up. "Help me!" I hear my voice echoing down in the well. "Stop pulling my legs!" I yell at my brother. I can hear gibberish, but I can't make sense of what he's saying. "Push me in, push!" I cry. Instead of honoring my wishes, he yanks me out.

"Why did you do that? I told you to push me in. I'm burning up!"

Si ignores me and lowers a well bucket (a five-liter can attached to a rope) into the well and brings up cold water. I snatch the bucket and pour the water on my head, and wash it off. *Ah!* It feels better. But I am still crying and shivering. When I look at my brother, he's rolling on the ground again. "Stop laughing at me. This is not funny."

***

Sage: [Mocking] Help, I am burning up!

Me: [Playfully] Hey watch yourself, Sage. It wasn't funny. I was on fire!

Dew: Aww, mean brother.

10 childhood stories: school days I

swimming with crocs and river worms

Our education system is as divided as the country is. We go to schools based on our racial background. If you're white, you go to the whites-only schools. If you are Asian or Coloured [mixed race], you go to schools designated for you. And if you're native, you go native schools.

The whites-only schools are few, but heavily funded by the government. Therefore, they provide their students with necessary tools for success — properly qualified teachers, smaller classes, libraries, state-of-the-art technologies, etc.

Next are the Asian and Coloured schools. These are not as funded as the whites-only, but they're much better off compared to ours.

At the bottom of the list, you have ours [the natives' schools] scattered across the townships and villages. These less funded schools serve the largest population in the country. And by any comparison, they're nothing like their counterparts.

For one, we don't have things like swimming pools or proper athletic facilities – just to name a couple. For a swim, we share rivers with crocodiles, river worms and animals that come down for an afternoon drink, or bathe to cool off. Okay, the crocodile part is an exaggeration, but we share the rivers with animals. Non-human flesh-eating, vegan creatures like donkeys, cows, goats, etc.

Learning is not always easy in these schools. Our classes are overcrowded, usually with forty students to one teacher. And to make matters worse, most of our teachers are poorly qualified. The *apartheid* law was designed to exclude them from the high paying careers. So some of them don't really wanna be teachers. They are only here because this is all that's available to them.

Another thing missing in our schools is the technologies enjoyed in the privileged schools. Our lessons are primarily taught verbally and through transcription on the chalkboard. And without visual teaching aids, we must rely on our imaginations.

–imagination (is more important than knowledge)

But even good imagination can only take you as far as it can be stimulated. Beyond that, there isn't much to explore. This is terrible, especially for those kids with a limited imagination. They can't make connections with mental pictures, so they can't keep up most of the time. Being a dunderhead is a curse; it makes school a nightmare for these kids.

Not all teachers are supportive, or have the "time" and patience to help the slower learners. Instead, they beat them, hoping that will resolve their shortcomings. And maybe, to cover up their own lack of patience and compassion.

Beating is their go-to solution, but it isn't the harshest punishment for these kids—the pain wears off within hours. What everybody dreads is the punishment that lasts for 365 days (366 in a leap year). What punishment am I talking about here? Let me give you another backstory before we get there.

Our school runs from January to December. At the end of the year, which is also our longest school break, we take our final exams. These are comprehensive — they cover everything we learn throughout the year. And, yes, we were expected to remember *everything*.

Unfortunately, these slow learners can't remember all that stuff, so the harshest punishment falls upon them: they're held back for another year. This is really stressful for these kids. They literally have to watch their peers move to the next grade while they welcome "babies" from lower-level classes. Because of that, it's not uncommon for kids to quit school and go work on farms. At least on the farms, I assume, they don't feel the pressure or get embarrassed or even beaten.

***

Dew: Wow! That was definitely different.

Sage: Did you really swim with crocodiles?

Dew: Sage, he already said it was just an exaggeration?

Sage: I heard him. C'mon Dew, have a little sense of humor!

Dew: Mxm!Anyway*s*, please take us through your elementary school experiences, Mr. M-Foddysumtin.

Me: Elementary school was mostly fun except for the embarrassment and the stinky corporal punishment we endured.

—the embarrassment assemblies

Every morning we hold assemblies where we sing our national anthem, and then teachers make announcements. Mostly, these are fun because we get to hang out with friends before school starts. But if you're late, fun is replaced with pain. A teacher will smack you in front of the entire school. Now *that's* embarrassing.

Speaking of embarrassing, there are these other assemblies we hold on the last day of school breaks. Not everyone is necessarily thrilled to have those.

Remember those kids I said always flunk our comprehensive exams? They hate those assemblies. And I don't blame them. They have a good darn reason to because this is when they really are embarrassed.

Anyway, nobody really knows how we ended up with them. But if you ask me, I'll tell you what I think. I think they're introduced just for these kids. I think teachers felt that sending report cards home without announcing the grades publicly was too kind to them. So one day, they came together with other school officials and said, "how can we embarrass these kids?"

"Marybeth, would you suggest how we might go about this?"

"Of course! We should interrupt classes on each last day of school and have the students sit crisscross applesauce in front of the office. Then we'll have all teachers read their report cards out loud to embarrass all the flunkers. And we can call events, 'the embarrassment assemblies.'"

"Genius, Marybeth. Genius!"

And that's *how* we ended up with them. Otherwise, how else would we have?

Anyway, just like Marybeth suggested in my account, we sit in rows and wait. Passers wait to brag about their accomplishments, while flunkers wait for their ultimate embarrassment.

While waiting, something confusing always happens. Every time I steal a gaze at these kids, they have their middle finger wrapped around their index finger. Now I know they're not all trying to go to the restroom. So I can only assume they are hoping their names are called along with those who pass with flying colors. But that doesn't make sense. I mean, everyone knows where they stand. So why cross your fingers if you know it's not gonna change anything?

Anyway, this is how it all goes down at these assemblies:

When your teacher calls your name, you stand up in front of the entire school. Alone. She flips open your report card and says, "Congratulations!" That's if you passed. Then she shares your grade to everyone's applause. On the flip side, if you flunked, you hear the loudest "FAILED" vibrating into your ears. After that, she tells everyone your low score to NO applause. And suddenly all eyes are on you, and you hear people giggling and whispering mean things. This is when we see people's eyes getting shiny, ready to tear up.

Once all the names are called, it's time for the special event: the ultimate embarrassment ever. All the flunkers are told to stand up so everybody can get one more good look at them. Then they parade around like a national team on the opening day of the Olympics. After that, they're ordered to sit in the front and face everyone. The entire school.

Finally, once they've had a good look at them, a class president is chosen. Uh...before I proceed, I just want you to know one thing: you don't wanna be that person! But if you're the most unfortunate person in that group, you're chosen as *that* president. A Class President of the Flunkers. And you are given the honor of giving a speech about how you all ended up in that position and how you plan to avoid it the following year.

Believe me. I repeat. You don't wanna be that person! And you don't wanna be in that group, either! But if you're, oh well, there's nothing you can do. The best you can do is to plead with the "mother earth" to crack open and swallow you whole.

***

Dew: Class President of the Flunkers! That's so funny. Aww, but that's sad too.

Me: Yeah, that's a title you didn't want to have on your resume.

Sage: I am glad I didn't go to that school, M46!

Me: Yeah, it was rough. January was the most intense time of the year, especially for the flunkers.

Dew: Wow! I get chills just imagining what it must have been like. Anyway, let's dig a little deeper. Please tell us more about corporal punishment.

Me: Sure.

—methods of punishment: the face warmer

Welcome to my elementary school, where corporal punishment is inescapable. A day rarely goes by without getting into trouble. No matter how much we try to avoid it, it always finds us.

This morning we are getting introduced to a teacher, self-nicknamed "the face warmer." I don't know what we got in trouble for, but we're in line getting our cheeks warmed up. I'm at the back of the line, waiting for my turn. But watching the kids in front catching a bubble and having it popped with a warm clap isn't fun. And the way some of these bed-wetters are crying, I am not looking forward to this exercise.

Ms. Face Warmer is the most hated and feared first grade teacher ever. Her thunderous claps leave kids feeling dizzy and disorientated. Some even report seeing stars and hearing a ringing in their ears. And the messy ones cry until snot mixes up with tears all over their nasty faces. Some are wiping it off with their palms, spreading it all over their face with snot bubbles bursting out of their noses. *Aya-ya!* Disgusting!

One kid is adding to the mess by puking everywhere and intentionally peeing himself. I guess he's hoping she'd feel sorry and spare him. But by the look of things, it's not happening. The tear-and-snot-inducing claps are continuing as planned.

My brother told me that yesterday two kids pooped on themselves and received more hot claps for stinking up the classroom. Then they were sent home to change clothes, but they went to the nearby river to wiggle it off. Apparently, they jumped in, took care of business, and then came out all refreshed. I didn't get the details about what exactly happened (in) there. But I can only suspect they left the poop in the river, still stuck on their underwear. I'm not investigating these kinds of cases because it's messy and plain-ol'-nasty.

***

My turn comes. She carefully lays my cheek on her palm - like a baby taking a nap - and with the other palm, strikes like lightning! *Ouch!* My cheek is burning and tingling. I make a big mistake by touching my cheek. But nobody told me I am not supposed to touch my cheek. Now she is starting all over again. *Aish!*

–the wooden chalkboard cleaner

The wooden chalkboard cleaner is used for offenses such as tardiness and noise making. How this works is, we bring our fingers and the thumb together. Then the teacher strikes them with the chalkboard cleaner. *Ouch!* This produces the most pain I've ever felt. It leaves your fingers feeling like they're broken.

To reduce the pain, we blow at them. Some kids even dip them in their armpits, leaving the room stinky. Some of these kids are really musty, I can tell you that.

Anyway, someone figured out a trick to lessen the pain. Now everyone is growing their fingernails. And yes, boys too. The idea is to have the nails absorb some of the pain. Apparently it works, but I never had time to feel it myself. By the time my nails grew, teachers had figured us out, and brought nail clippers to give us free manicures. *Argh*, teachers! Always find a way to spoil a perfect trick.

–pens and fingers battle

The next method I call "pens and fingers battle." I call it a battle because in action, it looks like our fingers and the pens are trying to see which is stronger. This is how it works, three pens are placed between your fingers. Then the teacher squeezes the ends of the pens together and slowly counts to five. By the time you hear "five," your fingers are painfully numb. And for skinny kids like me, the pain is more, because there's no fat to absorb some of it. It's pens versus bones (not pens vs. fingers), and the poor skin is caught in the crossfire.

–the switch

For crimes considered high level, such as stealing, the default method is lashes on the buttocks. These are special events where everybody gathers around to witness. They are intentionally executed in the open to embarrass the student while sending a clear message to others. The events are so well attended, you'd think it was the opening ceremonies of the Olympic Games.

The setup is: two big kids elevate the offender a few inches off the ground—one holding on to the legs, and the other vice-gripping the wrists. While safely floating, the teacher lays the skin-tearing lashes. All you can do is wiggle and wail as loud and as long as you so choose. Talk about embarrassment! If that ever happens to me, I'm hitchhiking to another planet.

–sticks on the palms

The stick on the palms is the go-to method. It's mostly used for minor, everyday offenses. I think that's because it's easy and quick to administer. Still, it hurts so much, especially in the winter when our hands are frozen cold.

But just as with everything that brings pain, solutions are pondered. Today some smarty-pants started spreading rumors, suggesting we all rub onions on our palms. The belief is that the onion will *magically* cause our palms to swell and teachers would somehow stop, thinking our palms are allergic to the stick.

Spoiler alert: Ain't happening.

Anyway, kids are lotioning their palms with onion juice before coming to school. But that's ineffective. The onion juice doesn't stay on their palms all day. This is a problem for them, but to me it's a gold mine. It's yet another business opportunity screaming my name.

11 my underground onions business

A boy's gotta do what a boy's gotta do for the bread- cha-ching

Now I've heard many rumors before, but none of them stood to make me a millionaire. So I welcome this silly one with a big smile. I learned a long time ago: where there's trouble, there's an opportunity to cash in.

After identifying my potential customer base, I bring a bag of pre-cut onions to sell to these crybabies. This is the group of kids who fear the stick that they rub onions around their eyes to provoke tears, hoping the teacher would feel sorry for them. But that's not the proper way to solicit sympathy. In fact, there is never sympathy. We all know what the deal is. You break the rules; you pay.

Anyhow, I love this crowd because they make good patrons: they're soft, always ready to cry, and most importantly, they're cowards. They'll never bring their own onions because they fear being caught. And that fear is a *gift* I cannot refuse.

My business venture starts off to a good start. But as the rumor spreads, more kids (excluding the crybabies) start bringing their own onions, which makes us look like we're attending a culinary school.

Within days, our classroom starts smelling like a kitchen. This is not good. These *losers* are ruining my business, and it needs to stop. I can't have these kids share their onions with my favorite customers. They must buy it from me. So I take action.

I skip the first part of recess and dash back inside while everyone is playing tag and soccer. I have a few minutes to search all the school bags and make onions disappear.

Okay, you're probably thinking I am a bad person for doing this, and you're right. But this is a lifeline my business desperately needs. It will create a need for a purchase, thus increasing my customers.

Once I finish, I rush back outside and join the soccer group. "Where have you been?" asks one of my classmates. I tell him that I had a little business to take care of, but everything is fine now. He buys it and continues to play.

When the bell rings, we race back to the classroom and get ready for a quiz. As soon as I settle down at my desk, I run my eyes across the room. I see people searching for "some things" in silence. Others are whispering things. I keep a straight face. I don't wanna cross my eyes with any of them. They're aware of their missing onions, but (we all know) they can't tell the teacher.

After the quiz, everyone rushes outside for lunch. The conversation on the way to the convenience store is about the missing onions. I join in to throw them off. "Maybe the teacher found them, and if you don't want trouble, stop asking questions," I suggest. "You all can buy from me." Surprisingly, a majority agrees without questioning. Well, the majority rules. So my business gets a second chance.

In a few days, I've become the principal supplier. I even offer credit for double the price to those who don't have money on the spot. Everything is going well. My business is thriving. Then one day all that changes. Apparently, while I'm on a restroom break, one of the crybabies gets in trouble. Knowing he's about to get a beating, he reaches into his backpack, (right in front of the teacher) pulls out a few layers, and begins rubbing them on his palms.

Of course, that got the teacher's attention and demanded answers.

In a last-minute attempt to have his penalty reduced, the clumsy loser snitches on me. Not only as the onion dealer, but as the originator of the trick.

Okay, if you're following me, you know that's not true! Right? It's a BIG FAT lie... told under an intense interrogation.

***

"Where are they?" The teacher throws a confusing Q at me as soon as I walk in.

"Where's who, mistress? (A reference to female teachers). I throw a Q back at her like a smarty-pants (something you don't wanna do). But the truth is, I don't know what she is talking about. She could be asking about anything: aliens, fat cakes or even her glasses, of which I don't know where any of those things are.

See, I was minding my business, taking a much deserved break from math in the restroom when all this started; hence, asking a Q with a pronoun leaves me clueless. So she brings me up to speed with the "Ooh-I'm-so-beating-you up-today" tone in her voice.

"Don't get smart with me! Where are the onions you're selling in my classroom?" she shouts.

"I'm not sure what *Mistress* is talking about. I don't sell onions."

She gives me the "I'm-not-gonna-ask-you again" look. Right then, I get it. Something has gone terribly wrong. I scan the classroom, looking for a clue. No one has to say a word. Just from the tension, I know the beans have been spilled. I'm in trouble. Big doo-doo!

But as a master trickster, it's only natural for me to reach up my sleeve. Unfortunately, there are no real tricks left. I take a chance, anyway. "Oh, those onions. *Mistress*, it's true when you don't sleep enough, you become forgetful. I totally forgot about them."

She gives me a "don't-waste-my-time" look. I get it. She means business. So come clean. But not entirely.

"Yesterday *Koko* sent me to pick up a bag of onions after school, but I forgot them in my school bag. And that's why they're here, safe in my bag," I say as I dip my hand into the bag.

Okay, I'm pretty sure the part about my sudden amnesia (forgetting the onions in my bag) is likely to save me, but I'm not sure about the selling part. And I can't come up with anything on the spot to justify that.

"Bring them over here!" she shouts as if I have swimming earplugs in my ears.

"Okay, mistress." I buy myself a little time by moving like a snail. The reason for this is because I still have profit *monies* in my pockets. I might be losing my onions, but I am not losing my stash. I've worked hard for it! Luckily, I have a way of making money disappear from my pockets, but still stay on me. So I transfer it from my pocket to a secret safety bank, a rip on the inside of my short's waistband. This is where I hide my cash from elementary school thieves and robbers.

Once the evidence is safely secured, I remove the *onions* out of the bag. I know I said there's no sympathy earlier, but it doesn't hurt to try. I'm the victim here. So before turning them in, I put on a show in an attempt to solicit sympathy.

"Hey, who stole my grandmother's onion? There were six onions in here this morning, now there are only five. Who did this? Mistress, please make them bring it back! I'm gonna be in trouble when I get home."

"Cut it out and bring those onions here! I'm going to pay *Koko* a visit after school!"

I bring a bag full of pre-cut onions to her. But as soon as I place it on the table, she throws another confusing Q at me.

"What is this?"

I wanna say, "Onions" but she's already mad and that would enrage her. So I keep my mouth shut and wait for the next Q.

"Why are they sliced?"

"Because *Koko* can't see anymore, so I cut onions for her so it's easy to cook without making her cry." She gives another look. But I don't know what it means. I can't put words to it. All I know is she doesn't buy it.

"Make sure you go straight home after—actually, wait for me. We'll walk together," she says as she examines the multi-layered veggie.

Do you know what's wrong with this picture? *Koko* didn't send me to buy her some onions. So there you have it. I've twisted the truth, trying to get outta doo-doo. But Ms. Noko is one of those teachers who really hates lies. Small, BIG, FAT, or white. All lies. So for now, I'm in real trouble.

***

Before I go on, let me give you some background info: my school isn't far from my house. And all the teachers know *Koko* well. In fact, the principal is *my people*.

Tick-Tock, Tick-Tock! It's almost time for the dismissal bell to ring. I keep my fingers crossed that it doesn't. But it does anyway. Everyone grabs their bags and rushes out of the room. I pretend to have forgotten her orders and tiptoe towards the door, too. She lowers her glasses, pressing them on her nose, and gives me a stern look.

Darn it, she didn't forget, I think to myself. "Have a good afternoon, Mistress," I try to play it off.

"*Hey wena* (Hey you), where do you think you're going?" she shouts.

"Uh... nowhere. I was just gonna wait for you outside, Mistress."

"Don't lie! Come back here and put these newspapers under the windows. We'll be on our way in a minute."

The newspapers are for cleaning the windows. On Fridays, the "good" kids skip the last period and clean the windows as a reward, while the "bad" kids continue with lessons. I am not always a well-behaved kid, but I am always enjoying the Friday break somehow. But because of this incident, I'm sure I won't be cleaning windows tomorrow. As I lay stacks under the windows, I think of puking on them so nobody gets to do it. But that's pointless. The office always has extras.

***

When she's done tidying up her table, we start walking to my house. Let me tell you something: walking with an adult who will be beating you later is not fun. I don't even know if I should share a joke or just keep my mouth shut. So I keep my fingers crossed like those flunkers during assemblies and pray that *Koko* is not home when we get there. But she keeps interrupting my prayer. "You know, if you had told me the truth when I first asked you, this would've been over with now."

Then she throws a tough Q at me, causing me to acknowledge wrongdoing, further digging myself deep into trouble.

"Why were you selling onions in my classroom?"

"Well, *Mistress*, I wanted money to buy dentures for *Koko*."

Did you hear what I just said? Yes, I said "dentures." That's all I could come up with. I know I didn't think this one through. Oh well...

"Stop lying before you get yourself into more trouble."

Did you catch that?

I don't get it. Why would she ask me a Q if she can't handle the *lies*? She knows I'm in deep doo-doo and I'm trying to get myself out of this mess.

As we get closer to my house, I look up at the sky and ask for my favorite get-me-out-of-doo-doo wish: I pray she gets struck by lightning and forgets everything. But nothing happens. *Mxm! Useless lightning!* I think to myself. We finally arrive. "*Ko-oh ko-oh*" (knock knock), she knocks on the front door. "*Koko* Mmabi, are you home?" She calls as she opens the door.

"Come in, I'm back here," *Koko* answers.

Darn it. I'm outta luck. As we walk in, I see *Koko* struggling with inserting her sewing thread through the needle. "Help your grandma," Mistress says. My hands are shaking. I keep missing the hole. *Koko* was better off doing it herself though it usually takes her all morning.

"Dumela, Mistress (hello, schoolteacher). Please sit down and have some tea."

"Thank you, *Koko*. I came at the right time," she says as she helps herself to the brew. "*Eish*, these kids, *Koko*. Today, I found out that your grandson has been selling your onions at school."

At school? She just twisted the truth. I don't sell onions "*at* school." I only sell them in the classroom. Big difference! If I was selling "at school" which, by the way, suggests the entire school, I'd have become a Trillionaire by now. But I am not because I only sold them in the classroom. Thank you very much!

"I've been searching for those onions the whole morning."

"Aww, *Koko*. A few days ago, my classroom started smelling like onions. Today when one of his classmates got into trouble, he started rubbing onions on his palms. So I asked questions, and he told me everything."

"Oh, my grandchild, but why?"

"He lied to everyone, claiming that rubbing onions on their palms would make them swell, and we'd stop spanking them. He spread this rumor so he can sell onions to them—"

Psst! Let me get your attention again. She doesn't spank us; she BEATS us. Big difference! Another thing: she's misinformed. I didn't start the rumor. And I'm not the reason the classroom smells like a kitchen. The onions are.

"—and on our way here, he told me he was raising money to buy you false teeth. But I knew that wasn't true because your teeth are still intact—"

"—No, no, Mistress, I meant when they fall out in the future. We always have to prepare ahead, right? Isn't it what you always tell us in class?" I interrupt with a smart comment.

"Be quiet. He's trying to change the story now. I'm going to get a stick and teach him a lesson, so that next time he sees onions, he runs away."

"Uh oh!" Whenever you hear a teacher talking about teaching you a lesson, know you're in real trouble. Right now I wish she was talking about a school lesson, not a stick on the skin. And what is she doing getting a stick herself? She's an adult, she's supposed to send me. Guess she's heard of my tricks. About a minute later, she returns with two sticks. "Mistress, why do you have two sticks? *Koko* didn't do anything. If you hit my grandma, I'm going to get the police..."

"Hush your mouth and extend your palms!"

I do as she ordered. Mercilessly, she lays numbing lashes on my palms, leaving them throbbing. I guess she's really mad because she doesn't stop until the stick breaks into two pieces. Then she grabs the other one and picks up where she's left off. Once she's done, she makes me agree to never do it again. I agree to close down my business.

I am devastated. But on the brighter side, I'm happy the punishment was carried out at home. Otherwise, at school, I'd have been lifted into the air and beaten on the buttocks for this type of crime.

With my palms throbbing and business gone, I have one thing left to console myself with. Once she's gone, I withdraw my *monies* and go buy some candy and bubble gum, and chew and blow my pain away.

Take home: Never lie. Lies will never take you anywhere. Be a cool kid and tell the truth! ALWAYS!

***

Sage: That was just child abuse.

Me: Yes, it was, but back then it was deemed necessary to keep kids behaving in school.

—enter*p*ainment

School is always a place for enter*p*ainment. A place where we get entertained [enjoy a good laugh], but also a place where we feel pain [corporal punishment]. See, we don't have options like time out in a corner or owing teachers laps at recess. For us it's a beat down. We are pretty much beaten for anything. From tardiness, to failing a test, to talking without permission. We even get smacked for giving a wrong answer.

Because of that, our classrooms have become a place where we hear all sorts of excuses. Kids come up with some of the funniest and weirdest stuff ever to escape punishment.

For missing homework, we hear things like "last night lightning struck and burned my notebook to ashes." The liar will swear by the lie, even when we didn't see a single drop of rain. I love these types of not-thinking-before-you-tell liars. They make my job as a lie detector easier. I don't even have to use my resources to crack their cases. I just check their shoes for mud. No mud; lies! And in my records, if you lie once - even unintentionally, you're a liar until you take your last breath. There's no self-redemption. You can't undo it. You can't un-lie. So these little liars wear the title forever. Anytime I hear anything suspicious coming out of their mouths, they're lying even when they're telling the truth. They've earned a "lifetime liar" title in my books.

Another favorite for kids is, "we ran out of candles last night at my house, so I couldn't finish my homework." This is the go-to excuse because we don't have electricity anywhere.

Not at school. Not at home. So kids try to take advantage of that. But I say no, not on my watch. After a brief interrogation at recess, people always come clean. And for a few pieces of candy or gum, I keep my mouth shut.

I've heard many lies in my life, but my personal all-time favorite is, "my doggy ate my homework, so I have nothing to turn in." This fib is on top of the "funny lies" list because it's funny and as old as schooling is. And I laugh at it, but when a kid I know doesn't have pets uses it, it's not funny anymore. It's straight up offensive!

12 an offer *I* can't refuse

I'm not a snitch, but don't push me!

As an extremely experienced, highly respected, self-trained lie detector, I take pride in my job. So lying about something you don't even have in my presence is a serious crime. Up there with treason! And I do not appreciate being undermined like that.

My work as a self-appointed in-school spy is always rewarded, thanks to the kids' need to brag. To catch these liars, I rely mostly on the word in the schoolyard. This is a great place to begin my investigations. So anytime a lie has been told, I go undercover and infiltrate groups...waiting for liars to brag about how they fooled teachers. And as soon as a boisterous culprit opens his big mouth, I nail that braggadocious liar on the spot.

Just today, I caught this kid, Jama, right in the middle of a lie.

"Mistress, I did my homework, but Sibi ate my book."

Okay, listening to this kid lying about how a doggy ate his homework is hurting my ears. So, I cover them with my palms to give them a break while he goes on and on.

This shameless little fibber is my neighbor, which makes it easy to tell if he's lying, yet hard to snitch on. But I can't take it anymore. So I write him a note, letting him know that while he might have fooled the teacher, he didn't fool me. I also tell him to never, ever do such a thing again in my presence. He agrees and proposes an offer I can't refuse: two pieces of bubble gum. We strike a deal. I keep his lie between us until recess when he has access to his gum.

The gum is the deal sweetener. The real reason I turned a blind eye is because his fat-and-lazy-good-for-nothing-sleep-all-day-cat is blind. Apparently, she'd gotten into a fierce fight with a polecat (skunk) over something only the two of them knew about. While she put the heat on the polecat, the gas master released some of his potent foul gas. By the time the slothful mouser closed his eyes, it was too late. She'd gone blind.

Now there's a rumor at school that rodents troll and tease her. People say they play "catch me if you can" in front of her, knowing she can't. Unfortunately, the poor old thing hasn't caught even a mouse ever since. The mouse filet mignon steak she once enjoyed, is now just a dream. Literally!

Jama says she often wakes up pouncing as if she's trying to catch a mouse, but ends up catching air. Poor thing! I even offered my pooch as a service dog to help her cross the road and hunt mice, but they didn't want to pay. So, no deal.

***

Recess bell rings. I follow him outside. It's pay time! "Jama, your secret is still safe with me, so let me have that gum."

"No! I can't give you my gum."

"But we made a deal!"

"I've changed my mind. If you tell the teacher, I'm gonna tell her you knew I was lying, but you didn't say anything. And now you're trying to steal my gum."

Psst! Yes, *you*, my reader. Did you hear that? This little fabricator just threatened to blackmail me, so he doesn't have to honor his part of the bargain. This ungrateful liar has the nerve to accuse me of trying to accept bribery after we had a deal. What a nerve! And to think I'm doing him a favor because I feel sad for his feline with special needs.

What he doesn't know is, you can't blackmail the master blackmailer. So, I blackmail him back. With evidence.

"Jama, a deal is a deal, man. You've gotta pay up... or else I'm gonna tell the teacher you don't have a dog," I threaten, pretending to be going to the classroom.

"Stop!"

"*That was quick*," I think to myself, flashing a suspicious grin.

"Okay, okay, don't tell the teacher. I'll give you the gum," he says as he reluctantly digs in his pocket to retrieve the gum.

"Gimme that!" I snatch two from his heavy hand and I throw them into my mouth and ask for more, "Hey man, you gotta give me another piece. This is a penalty for trying to stiff me."

"But I already gave you some."

"I know, but I swallowed them by mistake, and sometimes when I don't have extra gum in my pockets, I forget to keep secrets. So let me have another piece to keep in my pocket."

This is how I deal with wanna-be blackmailers trying to blackmail the master-blackmailer.

"Fine. But this is the last one I'm giving you."

I've never seen anyone so stingy. Parting with a piece of gum is like losing a brick of gold. Not impressed with such a level of selfishness.

"You ever try to stiff me again man, I won't be this nice. In fact, this is the last time I let you slide. Your accusations are hurting my reputation."

"There won't be a next time because I won't lie again."

Did you catch that? My job is done here. I just cured a kid of a lying syndrome. I have turned a terrible liar into a good, honest citizen.

But even though this is a great thing, I have mixed feelings about it. Where will I get free pieces of gum if he stops lying? *Arg!, I'm so conflicted right now.* Okay, I have an idea. Maybe he can be a mental liar: just think about lying but not do it. That way, I can still get some gum by interrogating him until he agrees he thought about it. Okay, mental liar it is.

***

Dew: Detective-special-agent-private-eye, you were a bad boy.

Me: No, I wasn't. I was just teaching those kids to become noble and honest members of society when they grew up. See, when you allow kids to lie, small lies turn into big lies later. And big lies ruin lives. That's not good for the human race. We can't afford to have too many liars roaming our streets.

Dew: Lol. What other kind of trouble did you get into?

Me: You know how they say, *an idle brain is the devil's workshop*? What that means is, when you have too much time for yourself - with nothing to do - your mind can lead you into trouble. And trouble is what I got into a lot as a kid. I remember this one time flirting with it in second grade. I don't know what had gotten into my head on that day, but whatever it was, it made me think I was a world renowned chef.

13 a fearless mother strikes back

Flying spinning kicks

It's after school. The Spring weather is inviting for an outdoor activity. It is also the day when grandparents are gone for the entire day to receive their government retirement payments. And my older siblings (the ones that are still living at home) are at school. So I'll have the entire homestead to myself for a couple of hours. "Hey guys, let's go to my house. I'm going to cook something delicious for you." I invite some friends for a display of my culinary chops.

The plan is not to go all fancy on them with a three course meal. No appetizer or dessert. I'll keep it simple and only have two items on the menu: one starch and one protein.

We pick up speed, and within minutes we're there. Before we get started, I make sure everyone does something. I might cook for them, but I don't work for them. They've got to work for their feast. So I send Roti and Lem to fetch wood. And Jay gets water from the well.

Once I have everything I need, I kick things off by making an outdoor fire behind our house. We have a tiny cooking room on the homestead, but I opt for open fire outside. It's more fun - like camping.

With the flames growing fierce, I fill our tiniest three-legged cast-iron pot with water and place it on a tripod. This is for our starch, maize porridge [cornmeal]. We pair this staple with different merogo [veggies] and dinama [meats]. I don't have the protein ready, but I plan to roast one of *Kokos*' chickens.

While the porridge is cooking, I huddle with my guests and brief them on the plan. "Okay guys, we are going to use a big metal bathing bowl to set up a trap. I'll prop it up with a stick attached to a thirty-foot long rope. Once it's up and ready to swallow the bird, I'm gonna make a trail with loose corn leading underneath the bowl. The chickens will gobble on the seeds, one by one, and before they know it, they'll be right under the bowl. Then I'll pull the rope, and, *Voila*, our protein is trapped. At that point, I'll slowly lift the bowl and one of you will stick your hand under there and catch it. Got it?"

Jay and Roti nod. Lemza, aka Lem, chickens out. "I'm not putting my hand under there. Why don't you do it?"

"I'll do it." Jay, the kid who loves food more than anyone in the world, comes to Lem's rescue.

"Thanks, Jay," I say as I make a trail with corn kernels. Then we wait for about five minutes but nothing happens. The fouls are not aware of the trail.

“Maybe we should just go catch one and drop it right in front of the trap,” Jay suggests.

“That is the most stupid thing I’ve ever heard, Jay. Why would you drop it, if you already caught it? Isn’t this trap all about catching one?” I say.

“Ooh,” he responds.

I just give him the “are you serious right now?” look. Lem isn’t that generous. He teases and laughs at him.

A few moments later, Roti gets our attention. He’s making his usual sounds and pointing. We turn around and see three chickens. *Shhh,* I shush them and watch the chickens gobbling their way into the trap. As soon as they are under, I pull the rope. One escapes narrowly and flees for its life. Two are trapped. Now it’s time to get our bird and slaughter it. But who’s gonna do it? I’m afraid to chop a chicken’s head off. And I’m not sure if any of these scaredy-cats can stomach that sort of thing, either.

“Alright, are you ready, Jay?” I ask. Jay says nothing. Then he breaks the silence.

“What if they bite my hand off?”

“Don’t be a *chicken*. Chickens don’t have teeth. Besides, they’ve fainted by now,” I assure him.

“You sure?”

Lem clucks and flaps his arms.

“Stop it. I’m not a chicken. Let’s do it!” Jay says.

“Okay, I’m gonna lift the bowl and you stick your hand in there, okay?” he nods. I lift the bowl; Jay doesn't do his part. "Why aren't you getting the chicken?"

"I wasn't ready.”

"Would you just stick your hand in there!?" I say.

Jay sticks his hand under without protest and starts feeling for the birds. But the fouls aren't having it. We can hear them clucking and shrieking and fighting for their lives.

Suddenly Jay screams. "*Argh!* It scratched me. He yanks his hand out, accidentally flipping the bowl over and freeing the birds. Realizing what almost happened to them, the fouls flee for their lives, *too*. Jay paces back and forth, blowing on his hand. It is so funny because he's so dramatic — like he was bitten by a cobra or something. Me and Lem are rolling on the ground, LOBO'ing (laugh our butts off). Roti is not laughing. He doesn't like laughing at people because he gets teased a lot. He knows the pain.

"You lied to me. The chickens didn't faint. I'm done. I'm not sticking my hand back in there again," Jay says as I reset the trap.

Who is gonna do it now? Lem has already chickened out. And I can't do it. I'm like a quarterback. My task [lifting the bowl] requires skill and patience, and these kids don't have any of that. So I'm out of the question.

We are left with Roti. But Roti has a speaking disability. The guy drools all over the place. So whenever he tries to talk, nobody can understand anything. I can't have him put his hand under there because the chickens could perforate it and we wouldn't know what he's trying to say. He could be saying, "Please help me! The chickens are pecking my hand!" We would miss that important cry for help, thinking maybe he's talking to the chickens in the chicken language.

Also, Roti is strong, and he's known for punching people when he gets mad. Understand one thing: Poor guy lives with frustration and anger from people not understanding him. And, whenever he's ready to release it, he pours everything out with that punch. So I can't let him be our guy and risk being punched by him.

Still blowing off his pain, Jay makes another suggestion. "Let's just chase them and catch one."

Without hesitation, we all agree. So we abandon the trap and chase the fouls around the house. After another unsuccessful attempt, we split up to increase our chances. Then something unbelievable happens: Of all the people, Roti makes a catch behind the house. We hear him screaming with excitement, but we don't know what he's trying to say. I can only imagine him saying, "I caught it. I caught one."

As he gets closer, I see all the reasons he shouldn't be proud of anything. This kid has a chick - about two weeks old - in a chokehold position. So much for screaming. Jay and Lem are now rolling on the ground, choking in laughter. I guess Jay has his revenge. Lem, I don't know about him. He just laughs at everything. Anyway, they're lucky Roti is in a good mood. Otherwise...

"Hey, what are you doing? That's a baby. It doesn't even have meat yet. Let it go!" I scream. Roti refuses to release the chick. While trying to convince him to let it go, the mommy chicken turns a corner. She's fearless and ready to rescue her baby girl with everything she has. *[Okay, I don't really know if the chick is a cockerel or pullet. But based on her determination, I can only conclude it's her baby girl].*

With her feathers fanned and wings whirring, mama chicken charges at us with ferocity and courage I've never seen in a fowl before. Realizing how much trouble we're in, we flee.

This is a weird turn of events. First, we're chasing the brood, now a chicken is chasing us: four big boys.

"Drop it, Roti, drop her chick or she's gonna perforate us!" I warn.

The kid I've never seen run before has opened up a gap, leaving us choking in his dust. This is weird but exciting!

I push myself, but I can't go past him. Roti changes directions and bolts towards the gate. Now he has isolated himself with his own speed, but the foul has her eyes on the prize. She accelerates and flies past us. Now it's her and her family's enemy number one.

Me, Lem and Jay stop to catch our breath. After all, mother chicken doesn't want to commit a quad homicide. She only wants to peck and perforate the boy with her baby girl in his hand. The boy who's messing with her family.

With lightning speed, the determined mother closes in on Roti, one step at a time. She's so fast, I can't see her legs anymore. All I see is blurry motion followed by dust.

Whenever you see a flight-less bird run like that, you know a school-boy is about to die. But Roti is my guest, and I wanna make sure he lives. Because if he doesn't, I'll have to tell his parents that their son's life was ended by a chicken. Now that's just too weird to explain. So I spare myself the awkwardness. "Roti, drop the chick. She's gonna peck you...alone!" Realizing he's singled out, and *el pollo loco* is probably about to do one of those flying spinning kicks on him, Roti drops his catch.

The mother sinks her claws into the ground and comes to an abrupt halt. It's over. Roti's life is spared. But he's not aware the chase is over. We scream at him to stop, but he doesn't. Instead, he speeds up and jumps over the gate and vanishes.

—chef de cuisine

After our terrifying experience, I'm still shaken. Nothing is going as planned. The maize meal is improperly cooking because I added the ingredients too soon – before the water was boiling. And the meat almost pecked us. Well, mostly Roti. Now I have a new worry: the whole thing stands to damage my reputation as a chef de cuisine. And I can't have these kids talk about me, telling people at school how my display went wrong. I must redeem myself and save my reputation.

So we regroup and take a vote on an option that doesn't involve a crazy chicken trying to perforate four school boys. With a stunning 3-0 tally, we vote for spinach. The leafy green veggie is in; the crazy chicken is out.

Koko's veggie garden is alive with all sorts of veggies. So I examine a few spinach plants, but right before uprooting one, I hear unwelcome voices. It's my brother and his friends coming back from school [guess they're on early release today]. Moreti is my third eldest brother. He's nine years older than me and he treats me very well. He's reasonable. Loving. And caring. I know he wants the best for me because he always makes sure I'm well behaved. So there's no doubt that I'm going to get a spanking if he sees this mess I've made.

"Put the fire out! C'mon, hurry!" I order my guests. In a helter-skelter rush, we get rid of the evidence like nothing was happening. Luckily, the time of the year is on our side. It's harvest time. Rows of corn plants keep us from my brother's view. They also provide for a perfect spot to conceal the evidence. "Go hide the pot in the cornfield. C'mon, move it!

Let's go! Chop chop!" I yell uncontrollably at Lem. "Jay, help me distinguish the fire. Put it out with water and carry the woods to the cornfield." Jay runs and vanishes into the cornfield.

After sweeping the ground, I dash to the cornfield, too. But as I approach, I am greeted by a disturbing background scenery: smoke is billowing from Jay's half-put-out woods. *This is definitely gonna give us away*, I think to myself. "Jay, the woods are still burning. Dig a hole!"

The only safe way to conceal the evidence is to bury it. So we quickly dig and bury the pot and the woods.

Once we're done, my guests suggest we all go back to my house. But I am not comfortable with that idea. See, one thing you gotta know about kids is, when they're guilty of something, it shows. And if you interrogate them, they break (too soon) and snitch. I am just not planning to have these kids get me in trouble. So we go the opposite way and leap over the fence and race off to the streets. Once we are clear of danger, we have a good laugh about everything. The chick-attack. Escaping the close call (clearing the evidence). But while doing our victory dances, Lem spoils the fun. He says he needs to go home right away. But first he must go back to my house.

Just when I thought we'd escaped unscathed, turns out there is a bit of evidence left at the crime scene. These cootie super-spreaders have left their school bags at my house.

This is not good. I can't have them near my brother. The only guy I'd be okay with is Roti, but he's gone. See, if Roti was to tell on me, my brother wouldn't understand him.

"Stop, Lem, you can't go through the gate. We have to retrace our steps." Lem follows my orders. He doesn't really care which way we go. All he wants to do is get home and eat since my treat didn't happen.

So I lead the group, and we climb back over the fence and dash back to the house. When we get there, no one is outside. This is great because all they have to do is grab their bags and vanish. "Coast clear. Grab your stuff and get out of here," I whisper.

Lem is in the front; Jay is tailing him. As they tiptoe to the front porch, the door suddenly opens.

"Hi boys. Where did you come from?" my brother asks.

"Fr-from home, I mean the c-cornfield," Jay stutters.

"What were you boys doing in the cornfield?"

"Um... I... we were playing *Hide and Seek*," I intervene.

"Okay."

Lem and Jay grab their bags and race away.

"Why are your friends in such a rush?"

"I don't know. Maybe they're hungry. I was going to, but the chicken tried to kill Roti..." (My tongue slips.)

"What are you talking about?"

"Uh...um... when we were playing, the chicken...I think it's crazy...it just came from nowhere and chased after him. So I told them they'll have to eat at their homes. I didn't want to have to tell his parents that a chicken took his life away. I think it would have been a weird thing to say."

"Stop that silly talk. Are you hungry?"

"I am, but I'll eat when Koko comes back. She's gonna bring me back fish and chips."

***

Phew, that was a close call! Once my brother is out of sight, I grab Rotis' school bag and bring it to his house. Roti is still afraid the chicken might be waiting for him at the gate. So instead of opening the door, he peeps through the window and makes his usual noises. I don't know what he's trying to ask, but I can assume he's saying, "Are you sure the chicken is not out there looking for me?"

"No Roti, the chicken didn't send me to lure you outside. It's safe. Let's go play soccer," I assure him. Roti doesn't trust anyone, so he stays in. I go to play with Lem, Jay and other neighborhood kids.

***

Later in the evening, when I get back, I hear my siblings asking one another about the missing pot. No one asks me, so I pretend to be deaf. I don't think it's a good idea to volunteer unnecessary information, especially when not requested. But is this a good idea?

Okay kids, PLEASE DO NOT DO THIS AT HOME. ALWAYS TELL ON YOURSELVES. TELL THE TRUTH BECAUSE YOU'RE A COOL KID!

—the ghost returns

My grandparents don't own a tractor. In fact, no one in the village does, except for Mr. Pete. Everyone calls him "the tractor man." So each planting season, every family pays the tractor man to plow their fields.

This year, we're first in line to give him our money. The tractor man cranks his engine and starts plowing. As he steers his Massey Ferguson tractor, me and my brother, *Moreti,* follow behind. Big brother carries a bucket, and we both grab a handful of corn seeds and drop in the newly plowed rows. This is unfair because we do all the hard work and still pay him. So today I'm going to demand a cut from his pay.

Anyway, about five rows into it, something unbelievable happens! The tractor backhoe hits and unearths a round piece of metal from the ground. My brother signals Mr. Pete to stop. The tractor comes to a halt. He picks up the object and examines it.

It's the missing pot! The one I buried months ago. I have forgotten all about it, but turns out it hadn't forgotten about me. Now the ghost has returned to haunt me.

My brain orders my adrenal glands to release stress hormones [adrenaline & company]. It's fight-or-flight time! My heart beats faster. And louder. My mind kindly explains what is unfolding, and what usually follows in such circumstances. My palms are now flooded with sweat.

You know when you know you're in deep doo-doo, but you still think you can charm your way out of it? It's that moment. So I try to play it off and go, "Would you look at that! It's a miracle. The pot is back. *Hallelujah*, praise the lord."

My brother is not impressed. The acting was supposed to deflect suspicion away from me, but has failed. My words have fallen flat. He signals the tractor man to resume. Mr. Pete revs the engine and resumes plowing. My brother hasn't said a word. I steal another glance. The words "I'm so disappointed with you" are written all over his face. Suddenly, he tells me to go to the house, and continues seeding alone. He doesn't have to say anything about the exhumed pot. I get it. My shenanigans have finally caught up with me. And nothing can save me. Not even a confession. It's literally almost a year too late for that.

See, the last time I got away with it because everyone assumed I was innocent and too cute to be stealing pots. But this time around, the evidence is clear. "Burying pots in the middle of cornfields, with food still in them, is stuff only eleven-year-olds would think is a good idea."

—my trusted go-to trick

I trudge to the house. I have about twenty minutes (of suspension) before I pay for my crime. That is long enough to prepare, so I reach up my sleeve for my special tricks for this event: newspapers.

Okay, I'm sure you are wondering what news has to do with this. Actually, nothing. The ink is rather useless right now, to be honest; It's the paper I am after.

Are you familiar with paper clay? If so, I want you to visualize it. Think of its texture - thickness and hardness.

Now, in your mind, shred a newspaper and place it in a bowl. Add warm water. Now rip it into tiny pieces and mix them until they're stuck together. Place the dough on a table and flatten it out with a baking roller. About two inches thick.

That's exactly what I do with this trick. Too bad I can't use it at school. There's just never enough time or privacy there to prepare. The only other thing I tried was the notebook trick. But that didn't go well. The book, unlike the clay trick, is not flexible and makes too much noise when the stick lands.

The next step is, I take the clay and wear it under my pants to limit the impact. Think of baseball pants with the padding on the backside. Got it? Good!

Now that you get the picture, I am gonna prep it before it's late. I've done this many times, so it takes me minutes to complete. Plus, I skip the baking roller. Instead, I sit on the chair to even it out.

***

Okay, I am all geared up–my behind is shielded with this padded impact gear. I untuck my shirt [to conceal the bulge].

The elders always order you to get your own switch. I always bring back the tiniest piece I can find. That way, when it lands, it feels like being whipped with cotton candy. Being impatient, and emboldened by my preparation, I march to the tree and examine a few sticks. They come in all sizes and shapes. I'm tempted to bring an entire branch with a variety of sticks. But that would raise suspicion. So I get the usual and return to the house.

A few moments later, my brother walks in and orders me to get a stick. I pull out the spaghetti-thin stick and give it to him. He breaks into pieces and says, "Get a real stick, or I'll go get it myself."

"No, no. No. You don't have to. I'll go!" See, I knew this was gonna happen. It's part of my kill-time routine. I do it hoping they change their minds about the stick and have a talk instead. I hurry back to the tree and pick one just about a few inches thicker. When I return, he grabs it from my hand, breaks it and does what he should've done in the first place.

Okay, you can't send a kid to get his own switch and expect him to bring the biggest thing out there.

***

I'm smiling on the inside. Can't wait for the "cotton candy" to make contact with the clay. I'll even shed some fake tears.

He returns with just about the right size. But suddenly he has a change of mind. Instead of laying the lashes, he talks to me. But this is very disappointing. I've gone through the preparation for nothing. Now I won't feel snowflakes falling on my behind. *Argh*, I am so conflicted right now!

After a long, civil conversation, I agree not to bury our pots and lie about it again. But I am still disappointed. I wanna ask him to spank for next time I get into trouble. But that would become sus, so I don't. Instead, I go bury the clay in the cornfield right next to where the ghost pot was.

***

Sage: That was wild, M46.

Dew: Yeah, that was really wild. Okay, let's move on. I can't wait to hear another story!

14 a lift to jozi

gliding like a pair of ninjas at night

It's June 1983, the last week of school before winter break. The talk around the schoolyard is about the break. Kids are teasing and bragging about where they'll be going. All the fun things they'll see. The cool things they'll do. And all the cool stuff they'll bring back from the city and show off on the first day of school. It's an exciting and tense week for everyone. But if you have nothing exciting lined up, you are excluded from the conversations.

The city is the place to be during school breaks. Everything exciting happens there: streets illuminated with many lights. Scores of strangers walking by and cars careening and honking on every lively street. Live music concerts pound from stadiums. Parks are filled with excited kids. And blocks of restaurants are oozing out aromas of delicious cuisines from all over the world.

To get there we either hitchhike, take a bus, or be shuttled. Hitchhiking is our last option. We only resort to it when we have to. The bus option is not our go-to because it only runs on Sundays, and we have to pay the fee upfront. So because we don't always have money, Mr. NT, a forty-something old man, is our best bet. But to roll with Mr. NT, our parents must arrange with him first.

Mr. NT's visit to our homes is as anticipated as the school breaks themselves. Sometimes it's more expected than Christmas, Kwanzaa, Hanukkah, Diwali, Las Posadas or Chinese New Year. The man is the most important person to us around the breaks: we pull weeds from his yard. Clean his big lorry (truck), all for free. We wish him good health. I'd even give him my heart if *his* failed. He's that important.

Today is Friday. I wait for him to come to deliver the good news. He doesn't. Mother didn't send for us. So me and my brother, Si decide, neither Mr. NT nor Mother, will decide our fate. We're going. *Finish and klaar* (period)! But to make that happen, we must first figure out how to add our names to Mr. NT's passenger list. Of course, hypothetically. "Maybe we can tell him Mother forgot to ask him to bring us," I say.

"That's not gonna work. I have a better idea," Si says, and shares his idea.

"But what if we see naked witches? I've heard people say they always see them running in the middle of the night. I'm scared of them," I tell my brother.

"Do you wanna go, or not?" he asks with annoyance.

I guess my fear of staying behind outweighs that of spotting old witches running in the middle of the night. So I agree with his idea.

—the plot

It is important that we execute our plan without flaws. So we use highly classified information (collected from previous experiences). For starters, we know Mr. NT's pickup routine: he pulls over, opens the canopy door and goes to fetch passengers from their doorsteps. He picks up his passengers on Mondays between 3 and 4 a.m.

We also know he's as punctual as the city bus. So we must be nimble; there's no room for sloppiness. Failure would mean three things: spending the holidays in the village, missing out on all those cool things in the city, and having nothing cool to tell or to show off on the first day of school.

And believe me, you don't wanna be that "loser." It's *that* serious.

Si's idea is not complicated. On Sunday, we pack a few clothes in grocery bags. When night comes, he hides them under one of the two trees bracketing our neighbors' gate. This will be the first pickup spot based on our investigation. Once the luggage is all set, we camp in the living room and wait for the magic hour. We take turns napping. I fall asleep first. Then my brother wakes me up. To make sure I don't fall back asleep, he dumps a bucket of cold water on my face. Before I could cry, he cups my mouth with his palm. While I am shivering, he takes his nap.

We do this until past midnight. At about 2 a.m., we stay awake and listen for our signal. An hour later, we hear the *Big Blue One* roaring as it barrels towards our section of the village. "It's time," big brother says. We have less than a minute to make it into the lorry with our stuff. "Follow me. Hurry!" Si whispers. We leap through the window to avoid our squeaky door. And like a pair of ninjas, we glide and take cover behind the tree. This is where we hid our belongings.

The lorry stops, but the engine stays running. As expected, Mr. NT opens the canopy and walks away. This is our swim or sink moment! There's no time for mistakes. So we seize the moment. Within twenty seconds, we're inside the truck, hiding in the cargo section where he secures parcels.

Now our only worry is nature calling. Earlier, when we went through our checklist, I suggested a few genius ideas. For *number one* and *number two*, I'd proposed we wore cloth napkins [diapers], but Si shot that down, saying we're too old for napkins. *Argh*, big brothers. I can't wait to see him wearing one when he's ninety years old, and tell him, "See, you're never too old for diapers."

Anyway, as for coughing or sneezing, I had suggested we bury our heads in plastic bags to absorb the noise. But he went against that wisdom, too, claiming we'd suffocate. I didn't believe him, but I complied in case he was right, just because he has a fragile ego. I had to be the bigger person for the team.

***

"*Shhh!* They're coming!" Simon says. The first passenger, Ntifi, hops on, wraps herself with a blanket and goes to sleep on the floor. Mr. NT drives off. My heart smiles. As we pick up more kids, the pile of suitcases grows bigger, burying us deeper. After picking up the last passenger, we ride for minutes on the gravel road. Then, the ride is suddenly smooth and soothing. I doze off.

About two and a half hours later, I'm interrupted by the squeaky sound of the big metal door opening. We are at

Bramley, a suburb of Jozi, to drop off the first kid. As everyone gets up, we emerge from hiding, too. Everyone is confused when they see us. We tell them we wanted to surprise them. They all buy the lies, except for Ntifi, who sticks her nose where it doesn't belong. "I don't remember stopping at your house."

"That's because you didn't. We were the first pickup," my brother says.

"No, I was." The girl is right. So the two argue back and forth about it. But who cares? I don't have time for pointless shouting matches. My mind is on the money I'm gonna earn, the cool stuff I'm going to buy, and the first day of school. See, last year, a new kid hugged all the attention with a packet of Romany Creams biscuits [cookies] no one had seen before. And boy, did the girls go nuts over those chocolate goodies!

Anyway, this year I am stealing the spotlight.

***

The lorry stops again in Norwood, another suburb. Two kids, a brother and a sister, hop off. Mr. NT closes the door, but immediately opens it again and takes a glimpse of me and my brother. He says nothing. *He must be wondering if we're supposed to be here or not. Well, too late now, Mr. NT. There's nothing you can do now. We traveled for almost two hours. You can't take us back,* I think to myself.

Mr. NT shuts the door and barrels down the streets to the next suburb. After dropping Lolo off at Linksfield, a beautiful neighborhood perched on a hill, Mr. NT invites us to ride in the cabin with him. "How did you boys get in here? Because I don't remember picking you up." I keep my mouth shut and let the "grown-ups" talk. In situations like this, I consider my brother *a* grown up; I'm just an innocent kid. So he has to represent the team. Si tells the man the truth. He always does this whenever he has no choice.

Mr. NT sighs and reaches into his glove compartment and retrieves a notebook. After confirming Mother's address, he gives advice, "you boys shouldn't do this again." We agree, even though we know we won't keep that agreement.

Mother works in Sydenham, another suburb with rows of big beautiful houses decorated with colorful gardens. And now it's time to face her. But I'm not worried. Know why? Because if she gets mad at us, I'll point at big brother and say, "this *man* made me do it." And if she asks, "Why didn't you refuse?" I'll say, "I was afraid he'd choke me, and I'm still too young to kick the bucket!" But if my brother disagrees, I'll say, "*Oops*, I must have dreamed it. Can we just drop it, please? I have the first day of school to prepare for. Thank you very much!"

—jozi

Finally, at 7 a.m., we pull over in front of a property on Raglan Street. Mr. NT jumps out and rings the bell. Seconds later, Mother opens the wooden, brown gate. They have a brief conversation. Mother rushes back inside and returns with her purse. She settles our debt and welcomes us gleefully. *I guess she's not mad after all. But I'm confused. If she knew she wanted us to come, why did she let us go through all that trouble?*

Okay, I don't blame Mother for not being mad. I am just too cute to be mad at. But I'm pretty sure she's mad at my brother; my cuteness makes it hard for her to express it.

Mother leads us into the property. Immediately, I'm blown away by everything I see. These people have everything: a beautiful house with a swimming pool, indoor bathrooms, and a fleet of cars. And their children, oh my gosh, they have lots of stuff laying everywhere - bicycles, toys and cool clothes and snacks. Anything fancy and rich you can imagine. These are things a kid like me can only dream of. *It's unfair,* I think to myself.

It doesn't make sense to me. How can one family have more stuff than a thousand native families have combined? I don't like this. See, before coming here, I only knew they had taken my mother away from me. But now that I'm here, seeing it in action, I hate it. So much for my first day!

After getting settled, we tell Mother we're going to Pick n Pay hypermarket in Norwood. We walk for about thirty minutes. This is the most exciting part of the vacation. We earn money there by pushing grocery carts for shoppers. And good money, too, if you have a natural charm.

Our first day goes well. I make so much money that I even start buying stuff. Every day, I go through my list and buy something nice and I save the rest of my money. My brother makes friends, but they don't hustle like me. Sometimes they disappear and I don't see him until after lunch. Sometimes, only when it's time to go.

I make a friend, too. His name is Raven. On Friday, Raven approaches me with a bag full of meat. When I ask him where he got it from, he tells me the truth. This kid is a meat thief. He steals meat packages from the shoppers. Usually ladies. He says it's easy to lift meat from them, because they are always worried about how they look.

"This is how I do it," he says. "I push the cart to their cars. When we get there, they sit in the car and put on makeup while I load the groceries in the boot (trunk). This is my opportunity. I slide the meat packets under cars in the next parking slot."

After bringing me up to speed with his meat-stealing scheme, Raven asks if I wanna try it. At first I struggle with the idea, but after his smooth pep talk, I agree to give it a try.

My moment to prove that I'm worthy of joining his meat-stealing club comes. I am terrified. I look at the lady in the car. She's doing exactly what Raven said they do. I lower my head into the boot and start digging into the grocery bags. I can't even find the meat bags. When I finally have one in my hand, the lady exits the car and approaches me. I panic and throw it under her car. But this is a big problem. She's going to see it as she pulls out in reverse.

I cross my fingers and hope she doesn't. She pays me and gets back in the car. Just as she's about to expose it, Raven pops out of nowhere and saves the day. He jumps in front of the vehicle and sits on top of the meat bag, which confuses the poor lady. She rolls down the window. "Oh my God, what is he doing? Is he okay?" she asks.

"Yes, he's fine, ma'am. He's just tired and hungry," I say.

"Okay boys, go buy yourselves something to eat."

Go buy yourselves something to eat? With what money? The cheapskate only paid me five pennies for my hard work. Now she has the nerve to say, "*go buy yourselves something to eat?*" For a second, I'm glad I stole her meat.

As she drives off, Raven gets up and schools me on how to do it right. We laugh about it. The store is about to close, so we call it quits for the day. On our walk to the park to barbecue the meat, I throw a Q at him. "Why do you steal people's meat?"

Raven stops, looks me in the eye and says, "Because these people are stingy and exploit us, so I pay myself with their meat. *Futhi, ngithanda inyama* [I love meat]."

But Raven doesn't stop there. "Plus, they have stolen our land. So when I steal from them, I take back what is mine," he asserts.

His reasoning sounds fair enough. But stealing people's meat isn't for me. I have to focus on my mission.

The following day, I quit hanging out with him and work alone. I continue using my less immoral strategy [today is my birthday] to get more money. The trick doesn't always work, though. Some shoppers are generous. Others are straight cheapskates, as Raven said. Yesterday a lady paid me twenty rands. Now that's handsome compared to the five pennies.

***

Today I'm buying myself a digital expandable watch. It's called "expandable" because you can detach it from the wristband and turn it into a robot figure. I'm gonna wear it on the first day of school. Next on my list are clothes and toys. No more pushing bricks. Also, there are these popular slip-ons called "ninja shoes" and a t-shirt with this plastic duck attached to the chest area. When you press on it, it makes a quack sound. I am *sooo* getting that. I will wear it under my uniform. And when the class is quiet, I'll make the suck quack. Nobody will know where the sound came from. But if the teacher finds out, and I get in trouble, that's okay, because people will still think I'm cool.

Tonight I'm looking forward to going to an arcade called Mean Machine on Louis Botha Avenue. My brother and I play games there every evening 'till late. My favorite is Rally-X, a race car game where you control a car and must clear ten yellow flags before running out of juice. All the while, you must outpace red enemy cars *and* avoid hitting rocks on the track.

Si doesn't care much for those kinds of games. He hangs out and plays pool with a group of white guys who call themselves "Ducktails." They are a motorcycle gang from wealthy families, just like my mother works for. I don't really know what they're up to, but I think they're cool.

***

It's been three weeks since the holidays began. And I'm so ready to go back to school. Mr. NT is shuttling us back home tonight. So after breakfast, me and Si tell Mother that we're going to push carts for the last time. "Make sure you're back by 4 because you are leaving at 6!" Mother says. We agree and head down to Norwood.

I spend the day working nonstop. I am done buying everything I wanted, so I'm saving every penny I earn today. A little after 3 p.m., we head back to pack and wait for our punctual driver. As expected, Mr. NT pulls up at 6 p.m. sharp. We bid Mother goodbye and hit the road. After picking up everyone, -in a reverse order of how we were dropped- Mr. N.T puts the pedal on the metal. In no time we are home.

I spend most of the time awake. Waiting for the first day of school. The morning comes and I load my new school bag with all sorts of things to show off. I wear my quacking t-shirt and my watch. At recess, I grab all the attention. Kids take turns looking at my stuff and pressing on my t-shirt. I can't wear my ninja shoes, but I have them in my bag to wear after school.

***

Dew: I'm glad you stopped hanging around that meat-stealing guy. He could've gotten you in trouble.

Me: I know right? And as for the meat, sometimes I wonder what those people thought happened to their meat when they got home. I can only assume some didn't realize anything happened because they stocked up on meat like it was going out of fashion. I doubt if they ever suspected the cart boy.

Dew: Okay, we have a question from the floor.

Trish: Hi Mrm46. I am Trish, and my Q is, did y'all bullies in your school?

Me: Of course!

While on this subject, let me make it clear: I'm not, in any way, glorifying or condoning bullying. Always speak out if you experience or see it. talk to your teachers and parents!!!

15 the bully

fearfully knowns as Big Pun

My entire elementary school has only one real bully. This alpha male (aka *loser,* in my eyes) roams the schoolyard boastfully like a wild cat, and totally overshadows his wanna-be copycats. His name is Art, but he's fearfully known around the schoolyard as "The Punisher," "Big Pun," or just "Pun."

Everything about Pun is ginormous: gigantic head, humongous gums and teeth, long bracketed legs with extra-large ironman calves, size thirteen shoe, super large knuckles - about the size of a big-headed newborn baby. A punch from those things would make your intestines flee upwards and take cover in the rib cage.

Big Pun is the administrator in charge of who can or can't be a bully. And according to his by-laws, only he *gets to be the* bully by default. He doesn't give us a chance to vote democratically for our own bully. Not that we want to, but still... Pun is basically like a dictator who holds elections and claims a landslide victory even before the votes are counted.

He holds a distinguished record of being the biggest, oldest person in the entire school - possibly in the entire history of schooling. He's been in elementary school for so long, teachers look like they were once his classmates. Undeniably, this is an accomplishment worthy of recognition. No one achieves such a milestone without dedication and courage. He's worked hard to remain in the same class, year after year.

The way I see it, "Guinness Book of World Records" is missing out on a rare accomplishment here. The man deserves a place in history. A mention in the categories of: Elementary School's Oldest Student Ever, Highest Failing Record, and Straight Up Dunderhead. On top of that, I think he should get his own personal phone on his desk like teachers do. I believe that's a privilege he's earned, fair and square. No one in the history of this school has even come close to that feat.

Pun keeps a legion of collaborators who brief him each morning, like he's some kind of president. These informants bring him up to speed with everything happening on and off the schoolyard. From fakers, pretending to be real bullies, to schoolyard gossip.

He has a powerful way of putting fear in the hearts of little boys. Only signaling his infamous fear-mongering gesture, the peace sign followed by a clenched fist) gets it done. People start shaking. The two fingers mean two p.m. That's when school is out.

Big Pun isolates his victims like a lion singling out an injured prey on an African savanna. Once that happens, nothing and no one can save the victim. The public poundings go on as planned ninety-nine percent of the time.

—catching a break

We don't have a cafeteria in our school. So kids either bring their own food, go home for lunch, or eat at a nearby cafe. Of all the options, choice two is your best bet to catch a break when you're in trouble. You just pretend you're going home to eat, but never come back.

Pun's Public Display of Might (PDMs) is inescapable, but there are two tricks that get people off the hook. Temporarily! The first, which is riskier, is what I call, The Disappearing Act (TDA). As the name suggests, TDA depends on one's ability to pull off a Houdini (a vanishing magic trick). But if you can't, well, let's just say, you're getting the beating!

The second trick is what I call, The Self-Diagnosed Patient. This universal trick has been around since school was invented. Nobody teaches it. But every kid pulls it off (or at least thinks about it) in their *edu* journey.

What trick am I talking about? If you thought, "faking sick," bravo! You hit the bull's eye.

This trick is our go-to because it is less risky. Good actors always pull it off and escape the pounding. But let me be clear. Again. It doesn't mean the offenders are totally off the hook! It's just temporary. Sure, they might fool teachers, but not Big Pun. NEVER! To him it is just a postponed event. Once the offender returns, the poundings resume, rain or shine.

—the same error

Today, this one kid got in trouble for something he didn't even do. Apparently, he'd left his book open on his desk and people, including our big dunderhead friend, copied his work. But when the teacher was marking our homework, she realized a pattern: too many kids had the same wrong answers. Okay, let's just say it is possible for a handful of kids to have the same wrong answers, but several kids misspelling the word, "disappointment" with only one "P" is a red flag.

Well, turns out, that kid had copied from someone else, who had copied from another student. And because the first student had misspelled the word, all these plagiarizers ended up with the same error.

"If you've copied your answers from someone else, stand up," the teacher gives them a chance to come clean. Nobody stands. Then, suddenly, one kid gets up and lies through his teeth. Basically, taking a wrap for Pun.

"Mistress, I copied from Art's book." Then other kids follow, "me too, mistress", "me *three*, mistress", "me four", and on and on they go. In the end, half of the class is standing up to save the bully.

I can't stand this. My blood pressure is rising.

These kids are guilty of cheating and lying about it to spare Pun the humiliation. Okay, I get it. And I can live with that. But what I can't live with is these liars undermining my superior abilities to distinguish a lie from the truth.

The teacher might be fooled, but not the good-ol'-detective-private-eye-international-secret-spy-agent, Me. I'm not impressed with that lame, under-pressure performance. All these kids are lying about the whole thing. And to be honest with you, I am getting offended. In fact, I'm insulted. Irritated! I feel totally disrespected. People are just getting too comfortable lying in my presence. This has got to stop. Right here; right now.

"I commend you for your honesty, but you all should have known better. Plagiarism is wrong and you must be punished," she says as she canes them.

Argh! Inexperienced teacher. I feel my blood boiling just listening to her. My heart is throbbing. I'm fuming with anger. *Sooo* disappointed with her lack of experience (in detecting lies).

Though she serves them extra five lashes (ten instead of five), I'm not impressed with her handling of the situation. See, the key to solving problems with kids is not about rushing to punishment. The important thing is learning how to detect the lies first, then give out a suitable punishment. It's that simple.

Er, mistress, can't you see these kids are lying? I know it sort of makes sense since the big guy can't spell anything right. But something is fishy here. And you should know that nobody would dare copy from Art. It's always the other way around. Pun is the only one guilty of plagiarism, and these little snotty faces are covering him. Do you know why, mistress? Because they'd rather take your licks than his pounding.

I wanna tell her that, but I can't. This is one of those rare moments when even a superhero puts his own safety first. I can't risk the big guy's wrath. After all, these are third graders;

responsible for their choices. So I keep my mouth shut, though my blood is still boiling.

Pun is exempt from corporal punishment. I think it's because he's [like] a senior citizen, or maybe teachers are afraid of him, too. Pun sits there and smiles boastfully as his minions are trashed. My heart throbs even more, yet I envy him. I wish we could trade places, so I'm exempt from the stick. Just imagine that: no corporal punishment, not even a reprimand. But again, I have a problem with what he's done to earn his privilege. Growing a beard in third grade isn't on my plans.

***

Big Pun is hard to please. Though the kid took the wrap for him, he is not off the hook. He is still blamed and booked for an after school beat down showcase. To his credit, though, the kid doesn't just accept the sentence and march to the slaughter like a sheep.

At lunch, he swallows his food without chewing it. I guess he thinks he's a cow. Anyway, his plan is to have the food come back out once in the classroom.

We go back inside. He waits. Fifteen minutes later, nothing has happened. Clearly, the plan isn't working. So he sinks his head under the desk to give it a jump start. He shoves his hand into his mouth and provokes a puke. *Viola*! This time it works. Puke splatters everywhere. Kids jump clear of him, "hey, watch it! Don't puke on me!"

The commotion gets the teacher's attention. After seeing the vomit, she sends Pun's victim to the office. We don't have a school nurse on site, so whatever kids claim goes.

A few minutes later, the kid returns to get his books. He's going home. Kudos to him. He's pulled it off, right? Not so fast! It's not how things work out here. Not with "our" bully.

Pun gives him the "go-home-and-get-well-soon-I'll-be-here-when-you-feel-better" look. We don't have those *Get Well Soon* cards. But I'm sure if we had them, he'd personally hand deliver one to this kids' house after school.

As the kid grabs his backpack and gives the class his back, I catch a glimpse of Pun. He's fuming like a lion watching hyenas take his catch and there's nothing he can do about it.

***

Two days go by. On the third day, he returns. Please tell me why this amateur brags about how he made it all up; how he fooled the principal into believing he'd been sick with diarrhea? Anyway, thanks to his own big mouth, now we're in business. For a piece of gum, I negotiate a "I'll-keep-my-mouth-shut-if-you-pay" deal. He considers.

But while the bargaining is in full swing, another blabbermouth spills the beans. Now this kid is useless to me. So I pull out of the negotiations and wait for Pun' school PDM.

***

Dew: Mrm46, that was not nice.

Me: I know. But it was just businesses; nothing personal.

Sage: Did you ever get in trouble with the bully guy, M46?

Me: No one was immune to Pun's PDMs.

—trouble finds me

Today is Friday, and our class has what I call the "Dictionary Test (DT)." DT is basically a combo of a spelling and a vocabulary test.

"Are you all ready for your quiz?" The teacher asks as she walks into the classroom.

First, we do the vocabulary definition, and once everyone has shown off their command of a language, we do the spelling test. I always look forward to this, not because I'm interested in spelling or definitions, but because this always turns into an enterpainment session. Thanks to Pun.

The English language is foreign to us, so mistakes are inevitable. The problem seems to come from phonics, thinking in native languages and answering in the foreign language. People rely heavily on the sounds. They confuse the sounds of English words with words in their native languages, leading them to explaining wrong words. But I like it; it makes for a nice Friday afternoon belly laugh treat.

***

A perfect example is with the word *calmer*, as in *calm*. In one of our native languages, the sound can be mistaken for the sound of a word that means to choke. True enough, my classmate, Lem, is asked to give the meaning of the word. Not only is he confusing the sound, but he spices things up with a little demonstration.

To showcase his superior command of the language, he volunteers me. The boy doesn't even care to fill me in on his stunt first. He just goes for it. Boisterously, he cups my neck with his hands and starts choking me. *"Calmer ke go kgama motho* (calmer means to choke someone)," he confidently yells to the teacher.

"Hey, what are you doing?" I try calling out, but no words come out. I kick and wiggle, fighting for my breath. Lem doesn't budge. He has me locked in a choke hold position for a good few seconds. The teacher sees me turning purple in the face and quickly yanks him away from me. Otherwise, Lem would have sent me into a coma.

So much for a demonstration, especially for a wrong answer. Anyway, this is still pale in comparison to what I face next.

***

Dew: Aww, Mrm46! Okay, what happens next?

Me: Enter*p*ainment.

—enter*p*ainment [the spelling test]

"Okay, class, it's time for your spelling test."

The moment we all have been waiting for the entire week has finally arrived. We're given a few minutes to showcase our spelling abilities.

As always, all eyes are on Pun. We all know he's gonna mess up and he knows it, too. Ninety-nine point ninety-nine percent of the time, he gets his spelling words wrong. Poor guy! He's not made for any of this stuff, which explains why he's still in a classroom full of kids young enough to be his.

As the teacher walks around, making sure we've put away our notebooks, everyone's attention is on Pun. But we all know one thing: never cross eyes with him while he's painfully battling with the foreign words. We understand that being caught with (even) a slight smirk on the face means one thing: The PDM will be on you, and ONLY YOU! Still, we wait with great anticipation.

We're usually given the entire week to study our words. But for Pun, that is not enough. No matter how much time and how many times he studies his words, he can never remember them once he's on stage. Stage fright gets the best of him, which I don't understand. He's a man; we're kids. Why would a man be afraid of talking in front of kids?

Anyway, today he's the first one to show off his spelling superpowers.

"Is everyone ready?"

"Yes, mistress," we all yell. Pun doesn't.

By the way, I have a secret plan to treat myself to a good belly laugh and still avoid being caught. So I will sink my head under the desk, and as soon as he opens his mouth, I'll let it out. I know this is mean, but it's our way of getting even with him.

"Art, the stage is yours," the teacher gives him the green light. Silence ensues. Tension builds up. Everyone knows what is about to follow.

"Uh oh," someone whispers, but we don't know who. The BIG guy rises from his desk. We remain hushed. You can actually hear a pin drop. Perhaps a sign of respect for the alpha male. As he drags his feet, restricted giggles begin behind him. He whips his head around. We quickly erase any signs of smirk on our faces. He proceeds forward.

Okay, this whole business of standing in front of everyone doesn't help. It makes it harder not to laugh at Pun. And easy for him to spot who's laughing.

Pun has a big, round bear face with rusty brown teeth overcrowding his mouth. Another thing that provokes laughter is, he already knows that we know he's gonna mess up. So instead of focusing on his words, he stresses. Even before he finishes messing up, his eyes pop out. He scans the room for mischievous behavior - anyone daring to laugh at him. And that, my reader, makes these tests special enter*p*ainment events. Something not to be missed!

Finally, Pun reaches the front of the classroom. He turns around and gives us a final "you-dare-laugh-at-me-I'm-gonna-knock-your-teeth-out" look. Tension and anticipation grow even higher. He looks at the teacher to signal he's ready, and quickly runs his fire red eyes back at us. Everyone looks around, pretending we're searching for something. No one coughs or grins. To Pun, any of that qualifies for mockery, and carries harsh consequences.

"Please spell the word, electricity," instructs the teacher.

Okay, in the big guy's defense, the word choice isn't fair because we don't have electricity in the entire village. The man probably has never come across electricity anywhere in his life. So how could she expect him to spell something he knows nothing of? That's unfair, but... oh well, it's showtime! A time for enter*p*ainment. A time to indulge in a good belly laugh, and pay for it later if you're caught.

Pun pops his knuckles. He does this every time he is nervous. Unfortunately, no matter how much I wanna stay clear of trouble, I can't resist the temptation. As soon as he opens his mouth, before he can even say anything, that's it for me. I dip my head under the desk and indulge in a good snicker.

The teacher notices I'm missing. But she already knows what the deal is – at times like this, I vanish from everyone's sight. She calls out my name. I remain mum for a few. I need time to wipe the evidence off my face. She calls again. "Yes, mistress. I'm right here."

"What are you doing under there?"

"Nothing, mistress. Uh... I'm getting my pencil!"

"Get out from under there. You don't need a pencil!"

But why is she yelling at me? Only if she knew how hard it is to be me right now, I think to myself.

"Okay, mistress." I raise my head out from under the desk, carefully trying to avoid Pun. *Darn it!* His eyes have been on my desk all this time, waiting for me to come back out.

Pun gives me a look.

Oh no, why is he giving me the look? I thought I'd cleared the evidence, but clearly I was wrong. And it's too late to do anything about it. I am in a big doo-doo now. But why didn't I get the fist gesture?

The teacher green-lights him to go ahead. Pun begins his long painful attempt at spelling his ten-letter word with composure, something we've never seen before. "E-l-e-...," This is super disappointing to me. I mean, what's the point of being in class if he will not mess up?

Then suddenly he pauses. The look on his face gives him away. He's in trouble. We all know it, including himself. We wait for that "C" to roll off his tongue.

"C'mon Art, you can do it. Take your time," the teacher encourages him.

C'mon Art, you can do it! Take your time! You need to stop, mistress. I don't know why you're wasting your time. You know this dunderhead can't spell that word even if he had two years to study it. Please, stop telling him that. You're just gonna get me in trouble. You know I can't resist the temptation. I wanna say this so badly but I can't. I just keep the thoughts in my head and listen impatiently, waiting for the big guy to delight me.

"...-f...," he continues. Bingo! We hit the jackpot. As always, Big Pun doesn't fail to treat. He just dropped an "F" on us instead of a "P." Once again, confusing English word sounds with native language sounds. *Ah*, what a delight!

Until now, everyone has restrained themselves, which is impressive. But with this double whammy, the laughter fest has begun. People are hiding behind book covers and sinking their heads under their desks.

The teacher silently asks him which word he's trying to spell. Instead of saying the word, he throws his palms to the side of his head and flaps them. Then he extends one arm, mimicking an elephant trunk and goes, *"Bahruuuuuuhhhhaaaaa!"* Please, tell me why did he do that? Because it makes him look like an elephant with one ear.

Now everyone is in stitches. Even the teacher enjoys a little look-away-and-chuckle moment. Pun has definitely won the "audience" with that surprise, nonverbal comedic chop. The teacher cuts her chuckle short and tries to help him. "*Ph,* not *F,*" she whispers. Art declines the offer. To him, accepting help in front of kids is more embarrassing than misspelling his words.

Now the class is rowdy. Laughs are echoing from under desks and behind book covers. Unable to deal with our delightful cruelty, he quits and storms back to his seat. He sinks lifelessly into his desk and sits quietly. The laughter fest ceases. We know the eagle is scanning the room for prey to take it out on.

—the eagle scan

The classroom is quiet once again. Though I didn't get the signal, I'm still nervous. The spelling test continues. One by one, kids go up and do their words. I do not hear even a single one of them. I'm too consumed with knowing my fate. And the only way to be sure is to do the unthinkable: intentionally cross eyes with him and hope he still doesn't gesture.

So before daring, I decide to check him with a side glance. The game plan is to go in slow motion, but return at lightning speed before he sees me. I take a deep breath and slowly rotate my head to the right. Midway, at about 45 degrees, I get a glimpse of him from the corner of my eye. He is busy scanning the room, scouting for another class-clown to warm up with before the main event. That's if I'm booked. But if not, then he's looking for the main event's victim.

I shut my eyes and turn around as fast as I can. I make it back safely. Shaken, though. But I still need to know where I stand. So I take another deep breath and prepare for another go. Slowly, I turn around. Darn it! This time, he is staring at me. Our eyes lock. I grin. He doesn't. He throws his size-of-a-newborn-baby fist on his left palm [like a baseball player warming up] and presses hard without blinking. I can't pull my eyes away. My head feels heavy. Then it happens. He gives me the ironic peace sign. And follows it with a clenched fist. I see fury in his flaming red eyes. "YOU'RE GOING TO PAY FOR THIS, come after school!" I read the words right through his eyes. He's still not blinking.

A tear slowly rolls down his cheek. He blinks. A simple spelling exercise has turned into torture for him, and someone has to pay for his shortcomings. And, unfortunately, that someone is me.

That's it. I'm the main event's victim, I think to myself. It's time to write my will and remind people to say nice things about me at my funeral. But my brain is not interested in that. Instead, it shoots a message to the body, prompting it to prepare for a "fight or flight" situation. But fight is out of question; flight is my only option.

My temperature rises. My heart speeds up even faster. Now my body is shaking violently, with my knees assaulting each other with side jabs. The next thing I know, my entire body is dancing in an uncoordinated fashion. While my body is showing off some of the worst dance moves, my mind suggests we try another trick. I take the advice and write Pun a note, explaining myself. *Pssst*!

I try to get someone to pass the note. No one pays me attention. So I fold it (to give it some weight) and throw it. Without blinking, Pun grabs it, chews it into a ball and throws it back at me.

Because Pun believes in being "guilty by association," everyone has turned into rocks, sitting motionless. The classroom looks like it's full of sitting corps. Everyone is keeping a stiff neck, facing forward and avoiding any eye contact with me or Pun. Usually gossip paper notes fly around the room, but right now nobody wants Pun's fury. People only move whenever it's their turn to do their words.

I write another note. But this time not for Pun. I throw it to my best friend seated diagonally to me. The message is simple: "I'm begging, please tell Pun I was laughing at *your* joke." The note lands perfectly on his desk. He doesn't move. Not even an inch. My bestie pretends as if nothing just happened. He acts busy without moving. I wave; he doesn't budge. "I know you can hear me. Read that note," I whisper.

My words fall onto deaf ears. This is devastating. What has this world come to when a BFF can jump ship and desert you, betraying a lifelong friendship because of fear? There is no more brotherhood. It's every man for himself. I feel abandoned and skeptical. "Humans can't always be counted on, especially when one is in deep doo-doo," I conclude.

***

The end of the day is fast approaching. I have no more tricks left. Nothing has worked. Still, something has to be done, and done quickly. I try to focus my energy on the flight option, but my mind races. I can't think straight. I only think of useless thoughts.

If he'd passed each school year, I wouldn't have caught up with him in third grade, which means I wouldn't have been caught laughing at him, then I wouldn't be facing his wrath.

I even think of my favorite get-out-of-doo-doo wish: I wish he gets struck by lightning and forgets everything. But that proves fruitless. The African sun is smiling widely outside. (By the way, just so you know, in case you're the judgmental type, I don't REALLY agree with the lightning thingy. It's just my mind acting completely independent of me).

Finally, somehow, I get my thoughts together and come up with a plan. Two actually. Plan one: I'll flee as soon as the bell rings. But while waiting, it hits Me: The plan won't work because on these days, Pun's informants make it their business to stop anyone from fleeing.

Motivational gurus say not to have Plan B, because it takes focus away from Plan A, but today I think they don't know what they're talking about. Right now, Plan B could well be the only thing to save my life.

Waiting is too risky, so I abort and quickly move to Plan B. I raise my hand to get the teacher's attention. It just so happens that she'd just asked if anyone would like to spell "electricity." But occupied with my escape plans, somehow I've missed it.

"Okay, we have a volunteer. Help your classmate," she says.

"Help what classmate?" I counter quickly.

"Didn't you raise your hand because you wanna help Art?"

"Yes. I mean, no!" Either answer is wrong to Big Pun. "No" can be viewed as not caring, and "Yes," means undermining him. I'm trapped, but I have to choose something. I know how to spell the word, but if I do, it will further embarrass him and I'll be in more trouble for "showing off." If I misspell it, I'll get the PDM for not rescuing him. Andt that wouldn't be good for me. I've got a reputation to maintain, you know! This is third grade. Full of girls.

***

I bite my tongue and choose to preserve my reputation. "No mistress, I don't want to be a volunteer. I want to go to the toilet. It's an emergency." I cross my legs and lean over and whine like an annoying third grader. "I can't hold it any longer!" I pester her.

"The bell is about to ring. Can't you hold it for a few minutes?" she counters.

Then I hear someone whispering, "*he's trying to escape."* That catches Pun's attention. He rotates his enormous head towards me. But I don't wanna see his ugly face, so I keep my head straight.

"Shoo! Mistress, I can't hold it anymore." I'm now hunched over with my arms folded across my stomach, shaking. That gives my classmates something lighter to giggle about. But the teacher insists I wait until after school. The only way she's gonna let me go is if I do the unimaginable in third grade: intentionally have an accident. Okay, judge me all you want, but this is a life or death situation. If animals can rescue themselves from a trap by eating away their feet, why can't I rescue myself with a little *tiny* accident to show how serious I am? After all, clothes dry off. Don't they? And it's not as bad as losing a leg. I have to get out of here before the bell rings. So I close my eyes and force the accident. But my bladder is empty. Seeing the distress on my face, finally she says I can go.

—the escape

I bury my books inside my desk. Slowly and carefully, I turn around to steal a last glance at Pun. Darn it! I'm greeted by his big, ugly round face. He is not laughing. His red eyes are glued to me, watching every move I am making. I quickly turn my head back, get up, and take my first step. My body feels like it's three times heavier. I can feel his fury behind me. I pull myself towards the exit. Once I leave the classroom, I stride past the other third-grade classes.

The bell ringer, one of the fastest kids, sprints past me. He's actually one of those kids that volunteers to help Pun catch escapees. And he's my track rival and a sore loser.

So, at the pace he is sprinting, I know what he is up to. Likewise, I know he knows what I'm up to. I speed up, but can't overtake him. He vanishes into the office and rings the bell five times. That is unusual. Normally we ring it six times, in sets of twos. I think this is a signal to Big Pun.

I dash past the office. I'm headed to the escape spot; a hole in the fence behind our outdoor toilets. When I get there, I immediately dive into the hole. But I can't go through. I'm stuck. My uniform jersey (sweater) is caught on the fence.

While struggling to free myself like a deer caught in a trap, I hear unwelcomed words. "You're not going anywhere! I've got you," the bell ringer says as he holds on tight to my leg. This kid has had beef with me ever since I beat him in a race.

"Yes, I am. Who's gonna stop me, you? Let me go so I can embarrass you again," I say mockingly.

"That was a lucky win, and you know it," he counters angrily.

"Just let me go and we'll see. You know I rule the hundred meter dash."

Between you and me, I really don't. We usually exchange the crown. Sometimes he wins (by a second), and sometimes I get the medal.

"I'm not falling for your trick. You're not going anywhere."

"You know you'll choke on my dust. Maybe your grandmother can do a better job. Why don't you invite her next time we race so she can do it for you?"

"Big Pun, I've got him," he screams at Pun and company. I can't see them, but from their noises, I can tell they are fast approaching. I twist and pull and kick. The kick loosens his grip. I yank myself through and put a burst of speed towards the nearby bush.

One by one, Pun and his minions crawl through the opening and give chase. The bell ringer is leading the pack, bolting like a wild horse. He stays on my tail. On the track we're neck to neck, but today he's eating my dust. I am nicknamed "Gone with the Wind" on the track and I am living up to that name right now.

Finally, I bend a corner and disappear into the bush. They do likewise. Their shrill voices filter through the trees. These guys are like forest people. They know the woods better than they know the palms of their hands.

Once I've lost them, I stop to catch my breath and have a quick prayer. But before I can say one word, I hear rustling leaves, someone approaching. As I open my eyes, the bell ringer is right in front of me, trying to grab me.

"You don't have to do this. Just tell Pun you lost me," I try to negotiate. But he doesn't budge. He's Pun's number one loyalist. And he wants to keep his name in Pun's good books. "Big Pun, he's here. I found him."

I duck and weave. To the right. He follows. To the left. He follows. He leaves me with no choice. I move in and silence his BIG mouth with a headbutt. He flies to the ground. I vanish deeper into the woods. Once their voices fade, I stop again.

I know Pun has nothing more important to do than to hunt and beat kids. So I climb and hide on top of a tree. Once it's dark and safe to go, I begin my long journey out of the woods. Luckily, I am not scared of the man on the moon anymore. I even use his light to guide me home. When I get there, *Koko* is asleep. It's one of the times when only the two of us are here.

***

Sage: Wow! M-foddysix, what an adventure! Sounds like it was fun.

Dew: Oh my gosh, Sage! Please stop. That was awful. That was really bad. [Turning towards me] So what happened the next day when you went back to school?

Me: I didn't. After two days of cutting school and hiding in the bushes, the principal came to my house to check on me. I told her what had happened. The next day, she put Pun's rule of terror to an end.

Dew: Yay! I'm glad someone did something about it. Did he get expelled?

Me: No, he didn't. But his grandparents had several conversations with the school officials. After that, he never laid a hand on anyone again.

Dew: Nice! Okay, let's take Qs from the floor. Miya, what's your question?

Mithraa: Hi Mrm46, thanks for playing soccer with us. My Q is, when did you start playing soccer?

Me: I chased the ball as soon as I was crawling.

Brie: Wow! But did you join a youth club or something?

Me: No, I didn't. I practiced every day. Me and my friends chased the ball every chance we got every morning before class started. At lunch, we just swallowed our food and hit the pitch. After school, we continued playing in the neighborhood.

Nothing could stop us from playing a game. Not even the absence of a ball. When we didn't have one, we'd make it from pieces of cloth and plastic bags. Sometimes we played a match with a tennis ball.

Dew: Wow! That explains your skills. Okay, we have another question.

Addy: Hi, Mrm46. I know you're so popular with kids here, but were you also popular in school?

Me: Not actually. But I did, however, get thrust into the spotlight after scoring a winning goal for my primary school team. As fate would have it, one day out of the blue, I rose from a spectator to a soccer hero.

16 making the team

goooooooooooooooaaaaaallllllll!!!!

It's Spring of 1984, and a big game day in the countryside. Students and the village people have come out in numbers to support their teams. Mostly ours. The field is jam-packed with excited supporters, standing on the sides of the bleacher-less field. Nervous fans are pacing back and forth on the sidelines, screaming at the top of their lungs. On the field, players are competing fiercely. The stakes couldn't be higher. It's the swim or sink game for both teams.

The referee glances at his wristwatch. *Prrrr!* It's halftime with a 1-1 tie. Players rush off the sandy field and make their way to their assigned classrooms. Our school doesn't have proper athletic facilities, so the teams will go over the next half's game plans there. My school team meets up in my third-grade classroom. The visitors huddle in a second-grade classroom.

Me and other enthusiastic fans join our team, packing the room to almost capacity. Those who can't make it inside stand by the windows, pushing one other for a chance to stick their heads inside. Everyone is into the game as much as the players are, if not more. It's a big deal, especially for our coach; the only female coach in the region.

She paces back and forth. She's a total nervous wreck and she can't hide it. And there's a darn good reason for it. Her best midfielder is on the floor, weeping like a baby because of a groin injury. His replacement, the only sub they have, is a no-show. Apparently, he has gone to help his father breed pigs at his job.

The whole thing is chaotic. People are panicking. Wondering. What is she gonna do? Could the team prevail with ten players? Or could there be a replacement to save the day?

"Coach, we need a midfielder or we're gonna lose the game!" screams Art, the skipper. The coach ignores him and continues pacing back and forth. Without a requirement for formal team rosters, any student can be deployed on the pitch as long as they're currently in school.

"Can't we pick someone from the spectators?" asks our center back, Biltong (Beef Jerky). This guy is nicknamed Biltong because he has long skinny dark legs that look charred—like beef that was forgotten on the grill overnight.

Finally, the coach pays heed to their suggestions. She scans the room, occasionally stopping as though she's found whatever she's looking for. Then, the silent hunting continues.

"Okay team, who would you suggest?" Without deliberation, half of the team points at me. My heart races. I have been playing before-class, recess, and after-school pick-up games with these guys since first grade. But never on the school team. I just never had the confidence to try out for the team. So their confidence in me makes me uncomfortable. "Why are you all pointing at me?" I ask timidly.

Her eyes follow their fingers and stop. She looks at me dead in the eyes. Fear takes over my body. My heartbeat picks up speed. I roll my eyes away and stop at the injured midfielder. He's still lying on the floor like a dying goat. *Useless! There's no chance this crybaby is going back out there,* I think to myself.

When I return my eyes back to the coach, I'm met by a flying uniform. "You. Put this on."

I grab the pieces and try to play it off by looking behind me, searching for the "You" she's referring to. But the "You" isn't there. I guess it's me. "Why me, mistress?" I say with a quiver in my voice.

"Your school needs a man, and you're him," she says with a commanding voice.

"But you're making a big mistake, mistress...I mean, coach," I protest as I put the shirt on. "You've got the wrong man, coach. Please... maybe I can be the waterboy. I'm great at giving water to the thirsty."

"Settled!" she interrupts.

The burden is on me now. I can feel my shoulders bearing the hopes of my school and the entire community. "But I don't even have football boots (cleats)," I say, trying my last trick to get myself out of it.

"You won't need them. Your people have been walking this land barefoot for generations. Your feet are strong as an ox hoof," she continues. "Now, go out there and help your team win this match. Kick that ball like you hate it. Kick it hard, son!"

Ah, you got jokes; I see! Without further protest, I put on the shorts. After the pep talk, we jog back to the pitch. Our die-hard supporters join us, cheering. Everyone is anxious because the big prize is just one goal away. The winner will advance to the regional tournament: The tourney where only the cream of the crop, the who's who of elementary school soccer, competes.

This is the first time I have been so scared of playing soccer. I feel my stomach disagreeing with the whole thing. I try to hide my face by looking at the opposite side, but it's impossible. The group surrounds us and shakes our hands as we jog. "You can do this! You're the better team!" Some offer words of encouragement. Even those who know little about the game have a thing or two to say.

Finally, we hit the dirt field fitted with two steel-made goal posts. We take our positions. Minutes later, the visitors join us and assume their positions, too. The player match-up favors them. Most are bigger, taller, and stronger. From a distance, they look like professional players. That sends a shock down my spine.

The African sun is still above our heads, roasting the sand. Without boots, my feet burn, so I dance around to avoid blisters. Oh, did I tell you I have a secret plan? Yes, I do. I'm just going to be a number out there. I will run back and forth but not chase or call for the ball. When it comes my way, I'm gonna kick it away from me as far as possible. That's my plan.

Anyway, the minute everyone (except for me) has been waiting for is here. The referee blows the whistle. The visitors kick-off the game. Second half is underway. My teammates, except for me and the goalie, start attacking. Instead, I move about aimlessly as planned. I'm pretty useless to this team and I prefer it that way. I stick to my plans, and move around like a grandma with a hip problem, carefully ducking the ball. But it doesn't take long for my non-involvement to hurt the team. My position has become the weakest link: a spot where the visitor's midfielder moves the ball unmarked.

One of our players tries to remedy the situation. He marks the midfielder, but that leaves his man unmarked. Everyone from my team tries harder and harder, but their spirit is slowly breaking. They lose form. Communication falls apart, too. But this sloppiness is perfect for me — it reduces the pressure on me, and it's easier to hide when everyone is moving in confusion.

Second half is terrible for my school. It's clear our best midfielder has left a vacuum in the middle of the field. And he's missed. Me, I'm just dead weight. And I am about to cost them the most important game of the season. I'm not in the game to win, but to prove a point: Coach made a mistake. I was just fine rooting for the team from the sidelines. But, *oh no, she had to bother me*. Now she will lose the game because of that wrong decision.

Our rivals take total control of the ball - and the game. They make great tackles and get close to net their second goal. But our goalie, nicknamed "The Black Cat" for his ability to leap, denies them their greatest chance with an amazing catch.

Our panicked supporters lose their minds. Everyone screams and whistles and cheers and claps, chanting his name. "Black Cat! Black Cat! Black Cat!"

His save changes the energy on and off the field. Suddenly, my team regains its form. Players start communicating better. They're back into the game. Our attacking midfielder, Dida, passionately known as "*Swatlhaswatlha*" makes his own tackles. The excitement and the energy level go up. The cheers grow louder with every skillful tackle he makes. He slices through the defense. Now it's him versus the goalie. The crowd goes wild again. He tosses the ball to his left foot and takes a shot. Unfortunately, the ball flies over the goal post.

All the while, my plan is working. I'm hiding well within the mix. It's been about five minutes and no one has passed me the ball yet. And I'm fine with that. I can't ask for anything better than that.

Then, a few more minutes later, some spoil-sport interrupts my plan. He calls my name as he curls the ball towards me. The moment I dreaded so much has arrived. I can't hide anymore. The ball rolls to my feet. I have no choice but to make a play. I blast the darn thing away on first contact, leaving my big toe aching.

Usually there's a visual follow up to see where the ball lands, but I don't follow. I'm not interested. All I want is for it to stay away from me. I limp away in the other direction. (By the way, Big Pun is the only person who'd once kicked the ball with his bare foot and deflated it without breaking his toes.)

The referee blows the whistle again. Coach calls me to the sideline. They've found shoes for me. I put them on. Even with them tied up, my feet still slide inside. I'm a size three, but these things are three sizes bigger. I drag my feet back on the pitch so that my feet don't slip out of them.

The whistle goes off again. The ball rolls from one player to the next. I receive another pass and get carried away a bit. As an opponent comes rushing, I quickly roll the ball between his legs - mercilessly nutmegging him. He loses his footing. On his way to the ground, I catch a whiff of his musty armpits. "*Ew*, what's that funky smell? Boy, you need to bathe!" I tease, pinching my nostrils together.

The nutmeg doesn't go unnoticed by the *now-alive* crowd. Everyone is cheering and chanting my name. The energy on the pitch is now higher than ever. We are playing our best soccer. We've found our rhythm; our opponents are struggling to keep up the pace. We play one-touch-pass midfield. Our strikers and forward wingers are slowly demolishing the visitors' defense. Ours proves formidable. Pun has organized the guys and built a wall too strong to beat.

The change in the game has moved me from self-doubt to confidence. I'm totally in the game now. *Maybe* even to win it. I call for the ball. Me and the other midfielders have taken control of the center of the field. The more we attack, the weaker the entire team becomes. The more we engage our strikers and wingers, the more their defense falls apart. It's just a matter of time before we dislocate it completely. With pressure mounting on them, they fumble balls. The team is now in disarray. They panic and start chasing us.

What's happening on the field is undeniably amazing. The beautiful game is at its best display. But the game of soccer is played to win, not to defend all day. Their defense is exactly all they're doing right now. It's just a matter of time before we take the lead. They can't carry on that way the entire game without conceding a goal. "Pressure! Pressure!" In unison, we do what the captain orders.

A kick meant for their striker bounces off his buttocks and lands right in front of me. Gently, I trap the ball, and spot a fast approaching opponent. Using my right foot, I toss it to the left. With the left foot now resting atop it, I guide it backward and make a nimble turn. The opponent slides past, barely contacting me. He can't slow down fast enough. He crashes into his teammate and takes him to the ground with him.

I give both of them "the look" and shake my head arrogantly. The wide grin on my face sends them a condescending message. Squinting my eyes, I raise my head and get a quick measurement of the goal post distance. Then I roll the ball slightly forward to a send-off position. No one is quick enough to interrupt. Again, (this time intentionally) I blast the thing off, sending it flying towards their goal post. "*Oh, no*!" I cry. There's trouble on my end. Not only has the ball left my foot, but something else is flying right behind it. "*Darn it!* Whose are these? Bigfoot's?" I whisper as the boot strikes a player's head.

Bigfoot's boot victim tries to get the referee's attention. No success. The ref missed the strike, so no penalty for me. The player is furious. He grabs the boot and throws it back at me. Unfortunately for him [fortunately for me], the ref catches the action. He blows the whistle and reaches into his pocket and gives him the yellow card. He only orders me to keep my boots on my feet. The player protests angrily. "Why am I getting the yellow card? You should give him a red card. He hit me with his boot!"

The ref turns to me. “Is it true? Did you throw your boot at him?”

I like how he asks the question. Because I did not literally throw the boot, I can confidently disagree. I roll my eyes, “Ref, I don’t know what this crybaby is talking about. When did I hit him? Did you see it, ref?”

“No, I didn’t.”

“Okay, then. Let’s play some ball and stop crying.” I order with a smirk on my face.

“Keep your boots on your feet. If I hear another complaint, you’ll get a red card!” he screams unnecessarily.

Knowing I have no control over them, I do the opposite: I throw them to the sideline and go barefoot for the rest of the game. But I’m not done with the crybaby. So I mock him when the ref has his back against us. *“Waah!”*

Okay, I know you’re probably thinking I’m being a jerk. You’re right. But it’s a strategy. The player at the heart of this commotion is one of their best midfielders, the game’s engine. So getting under his skin would send their whole team into complete disarray.

With a few minutes left in the game, I get another pass — my last pass of the match. I make a few tackles past two opponents. Then I take on their defense. Their right-back winger approaches fast. The right winger can’t run fast enough. I easily go past their center back. Now it’s me versus the goalie. The keeper makes the big mistake of leaving his goal post empty, trying to tackle me. Effortlessly, I go past him. Now it’s me and the open post. I blast the ball hard. It hits the top of the post and comes back to me.

But this time I meet it midair and send it in with a head trick. "Gooooooaaaaaaal. Gooooooaaaaaaal. Goal. Goal!

We've taken a lead with minutes left. The supporters lose their minds one more time. People are rushing on the pitch. After a few seconds of celebration, the ref orders the ecstatic crowd away. The match resumes. The chanting supporters scream at the ref. "Time! Check the time, Mr. ref!"

The match official ignores them for a few ticks. Then, looks at his timepiece and pushes a knob on the side. Everyone on our side- players and supporters- holds their breath. We're all waiting for the whistle to go off. "FWEET" "FWEET" "FWEET"! Three times he blows!

That's it! It's the final whistle of the game that would secure a spot for me on the team.

The fans rush back on the field and carry me up and toss me in the sky as they chant with joy and pride. I've never been a hero before, but I gotta tell you this. I'm enjoying every second. The losers walk off the field defeated and walking like mummies. Some are even shedding tears.

As soon as we make it back to the classroom, we are greeted by a group of animated fans. I spot some school officials, including the principal, cheering in the background. This is amazing! I never thought that the principal (who once refused to release my entertainers at 10 a.m.) would become a fan of mine. Anyway, I'm enjoying every moment of this.

I don't like the attention, but today is different. Everywhere I look, people are praising me. "We knew you could do it, man, we knew it!" I know they're lying, but I don't care. It's my moment, so I enjoy it while it lasts.

Overwhelmed with joy and pride, Coach offers me a starting position. I am the hero everybody needed on the field. But the real hero is Coach for taking a chance on a barefooted player who'd never played organized soccer before. And that begins my soccer journey all the way to college.

***

Sage: Awesome. Can't wait for the next story!

Me: Can't wait to tell. It's actually two stories interwoven. One fictional, one true.

17/18 the silent rider/Jojo & Grace

Jojo: Oh Grace, you gotta watch this DOCU, Life after Humans. It's so crazy, bruh! Okay, so after the humans disappear, dogs become homeless. No more organic meals and gourmet cheesecakes. They have to feed themselves, but they can't open their canned foods. Cannibals eat everyone, then each other... til the last man standing eats himself. You gotta watch it, G. It's really thought provoking. [Grace shakes her head]

Crack a whip, Dambuka! This guy never listens to anyone unless you tell him to crack a whip. *Wah-push*! Terrified by the mind-numbing sound, the sisters break into a mad gallop.

It's around 4 p.m. when I see my brother's friends riding on a donkey-drawn carriage. They head the opposite direction, but I have some time to waste before a scrimmage. So I grab my soccer ball and whistle at the animals. They come to a standstill.

"Hey guys, can I come along?"

"Don't you have soccer to play? I don't like riding with kids."

"Hey, Dambuka, leave him alone. *A re vaye, ntwana* (Let's go, boy!)" says the driver, Bomboya.

"Okay kid, but you're gonna have to unload these bags when we get to the mill," Dambuka says.

I hop on, but there's a problem aboard: The seat can only accommodate two riders. "Can you move over so I can sit down?" Instead of moving over, Dambuka launches into this unnecessary speech about how young boys shouldn't sit on seats, and how when he was my age he always sat on the floors... blah blah blah.

This guy is only seventeen. That's just six years older than me, which means we are in the same generation. So technically, we're the same age. But Dambuka has a superiority problem. Just because he's obese and lazy, he likes to act old. He thinks he's some kind of man with responsibilities. But between me and you, he's not.

The guy is the most irresponsible person in the world. All he ever does is cut classes and ride donkeys. Now, if you ask me, this is one of those people that is headed nowhere in life. You know who I'm talking about? The Mr-know-it-all*s*. The never-ask-for-help-when-they-don't-know*s*.

"Relax Dambuka, no need to be rude," I tell him.

"Tell me something, Youngblood. Have you ever seen a three-seater sports car?"

"No."

"That's because there is none. Now, sit down and..."

"But this is not a sports car," I fire back.

"It is. It's a sports wagon!" he yells.

I know he didn't just call this-old-beat-up-donkey-drawn piece of junk a sports wagon! I think to myself. Okay, my dear reader, there are times when you must argue, but also, there are times when you must let it go. And this is one of those moments when you just zip it.

"Giddy-up, donkeys. Let's go!" Bomboya shouts.

"Move it, you lazy asses." Dambuka cries as he snaps his whip lightly in the sky. The siblings speed up. I can't see them, but I feel the tension. My mind drifts away. I imagine them having a little chit chat about the whip cracking.

***

Grace: C'mon, Jojo, you heard the [hu]man. Go faster!

Jojo: [Ignoring Grace] Oh no, he didn't! I know he didn't just call us lazy asses? Nobody talks to me like that, Grace. Nobody!

Grace: And what are you gonna do about it, Jojo? Ask him to stop?

"Er... excuse me, Mr. Human Sir, did you really have to call us lazy asses?"

Oh, wait... I almost forgot. You don't speak Qing Qong and the humans don't speak Donkey. So there'll never be a conversation between...

Jojo: [Interrupting] Oh yes, there will be... between my hoof and his potbelly. Looking like a pear, with a tiny head and a beer belly. "Say it again, round face! I double dare you! "

[Grace chortles as she picks up speed. Jojo continues]

Jojo: And FYI Gracie, the language is called Jul'h, not Qing Qong.

Grace: Jojo, are you a donkey or a linguist?

Jojo: Gracie, I'm a sophisticated linguist with natural faculties.

Grace: Okay, miss sophisticated linguist, how do you know Qing Qong?

Jojo: [Interrupting again] Juh'l Grace, Juh'l! Your ignorance is going to gimme a heart attack one day.

Anyway, I learned Juh' l when I was auditioning for "The Gods Must Be Crazy."

Grace: [Shaking her head] Jojo, don't you ever get tired of lying? You did not audition for "Gods Must Be Crazy!"

Jojo: Yes, I did, too! Would you stop hating! Just listen and learn, Gracie. "Qing qong qong qing xi chi." That means "Say it again, round face, and I'll burst open your potbelly like a piñata. Dad bod!"

Grace: [Shaking her head again] You're just making up stuff, Jojo. And you definitely can't do the clicks.

Jojo: And you're hating because I have swag and you're just a salty country girl with no dreams.

Grace: Dreams?

***

"Know what? Never mind, Dambuka. You win." I become "the bigger person" and find myself a spot to sit. The wagon is an eight by twelve foot flatbed with wooden rails on each side. Lain across the floor are two 100 kg bags of corn. There's literally nowhere to sit. So I sit on top of the bag, closer to the back edge, and rest my arm on the rail. Without a gate, I ride with my feet dangling.

"Let's go, donkeys," Dambuka yells as he cracks his whip again. Impetuously, Jojo responds with a hard kick, but misses the target.

***

Jojo: [Screaming] OUCH, I kicked the wagon. I think I broke something, Grace! I can't feel my legs!

Grace: Oh stop it, cry baby!

Jojo: Make me!

Grace: Make me? What are you? A third grader? You can't say, make me. You're a hairy teenager.

Jojo: Watch your mouth, Grace. I shaved this morning.

Grace: [Laughing] Shaved what? Your chest is still hairy.

Jojo: That's not a nice thing to say to a lady!

Grace: [Laughing hard] A lady? Now, you're a lady?

Jojo: [Ignoring Grace's question] Please hold me, Grace. I see dead donkeys.

Grace: It's, "I see dead people," Miss Know-Everything, not dead donkeys!

Jojo: Okay. Hold me, Grace. I see dead potbellies and spare tires.

Grace: You're being such a drama queen right now. Just stop it already and keep up before you get me in trouble.

Jojo: [Annoyed] Trouble? Are you kidding me right now? Here I am, telling you I'm dying because I kicked the stupid wagon and all you're worried about is yourself and your stupid trouble. I can't believe you right now! What kind of sister are you?

Grace: A big sister with responsibilities. And I'm trying to keep you out of trouble.

Jojo: Forget you, Grace. And FYI, just because you came out first, means nothing. In case you didn't know, I pushed you out of mom's tummy because I thought you were dead. And you know me, Gracie, "No dead donkeys left behind."

Grace: Whatever, Jojo. I saw mom and dad first, so I'm the oldest.

Jojo: Older! It's only the two of us, slow one!

Grace: Mxm! Are you an English professor now?

Jojo: The word is lịtterateur, my illiterate sister from the same mother.

***

"Move it, lazy donkeys. C'mon, let's go." Dambuka cracks another whip.

***

Jojo: Oh shush it, potbelly! Know what, Grace? I'm tired of this. I'm sick and tired of you and your humans telling me what to do; treating me like I am some kind of a draft breed or thoroughbred horse. I am not, Grace! I am not! And, in case you've forgotten, you're not, either. We are donkeys. Asses. "Hee-haw!" And this pulling and running... totally not for me. I wasn't designed to do hard labor. I am too woke to accept this injustice!

[After a brief pause]

You know, I was just perusing the encyclopedia the other day, and I found out that humans have been enslaving us like this since 4000 B.C.E. Can you believe that? Now that's too long to do stupid things for two legged creatures who can't even outrun a hyena. And that track star is different, okay. He grew up on curry goat stew. That's why he's the G.O.A.T.

Grace: A goat runs track?

Jojo: Grace, g.o.a.t means greatest of all time!

[Grace ignores Jojo]

Jojo: Grace, did you hear me? Did you hear what I said about our history? Know what, never mind. I'm pretty sure you don't know what an encyclopedia is...

Grace: I don't care about your ENCLOPEDIA.

Jojo: See what I mean? Not "enclopedia," Grace. Encyclopedia! E.N.C.Y.C.L.O.... know what, never mind.

Grace: You don't know how to spell it, professor?

Jojo: I can spell anything, Grace. I'm a spelling bee champion. Four years in a row. I just don't have the time right now. I wanna tell you more about your cousins and why they were meant for hard labor, okay?!

Grace: [Sarcastically] Hahaha! I believe you, Jojo!

Jojo: Don't get smart with me, Gracie. Watch your mouth! Anyway, when you wake up on Saturday morning, come watch TV—

Grace: [Laughing] TV? You watch TV? Jojo, you're a donkey, remember? "Hee-haw!" Donkeys don't watch TV.

Jojo: Okay hold it right there, Miss Smarty-pants, there's no rule that says who can or can't watch TV. Anyone with eyes can watch it. Why do you think owls stay up all night with their big eyes wide open? Huh?

Grace: I don't know.

Jojo: That's because they're waiting for "The Daily Show with Trevor Noah" to come on.

Grace: You're going crazy, Jojo.

Jojo: Gracie, you need to loosen up a bit and enjoy life like me. Be what humans call a "Couch Potato, a Show Binger!" Enjoy free cable; thousands of shows. Courtesy of the humans. Life's too long to be an unsophisticated and a boring donkey, G. Shape-shift or something.

Grace: I don't have time for your crazy talk, Jojo.

Jojo: [Ignoring Grace] Anyways, as I was saying, watch this show called "Horse Racing At The Race Track" and you'll know what I'm talking about. Your cousins are happy to be abused, Grace. Actually, I take that back. Your dumb cousins are abused, but they don't even know it. You know why? Because they're not thinkers, Grace. They're just low IQ animals who are glad to run around and please humans.

Grace: Blah. Blah. Blah!

Jojo: Don't you blah blah me, Grace. I blah blah you!

[Grace yawns]

Jojo: Fake yawn again, Grace. I double dare you!

[Grace ignores Jojo]

Jojo: That's what I thought. Anyway, wanna know what happens at the racetracks?

***

Up to this far, the ride has been pretty smooth. I let go of the side rail and move over to the middle of the wagon. Occasionally, I wave at passersby, slowly disappearing into a cloud of dust billowing behind us. But this isn't the adventure I'm seeking. The animals are moving a bit too slow for my liking. I want some speed. Thrill. Some acceleration. "Hey Dambuka, put the pedal to the metal. Make 'em fly!"

***

Grace: Go ahead, Miss Know It All.

Jojo: Thanks, Grace. No one calls me nice things like that. Donkeys are jealous nowadays. Anyway, your cousins give these tiny men piggyback rides, and chase a carrot all day long.

Grace: Why?

Jojo: That's because they only weigh twenty pounds. Hehehe, I am the G.O.A.T of comedy.

Grace: Mxm! Get over yourself. And what's with the carrot?

Jojo: The carrot is a trick, dunderhead. It makes them race without knowing.

Grace: Wanna keep talking to me, stop insulting me.

Jojo: C'mon, G, we're siblings. Siblings insult each other all the time. But don't you dare!

Grace: Mxm! What else happens?

Jojo: Gambling. Illegal gambling, Grace! Humans wear oversized straw hats, fancy clothes and bet money on these idiots. They literally get rich on your cousin's stupidity. And I'm talking millions here. Millions! And what do these losers get? A stale carrot and a brush on their backs. Not even acupressure or steam therapy. Argh, I despise those good-for-nothing- but-please-humans-all-day losers. Know what they're like? Canis lupus familiaris

Grace: What's that?

Jojo: Dogs, Grace! They're just like dogs. Argh, I can't stand those little annoying creatures. You know what their problem is, Grace? They think they're human. That's their problem!

Ever since they started living indoors with the bipeds, eating organic vegan diet and riding in cars, sticking their tongues and ugly faces out the windows, they think they're all that. Oh, I can't stand 'em, G. Just last week, I was minding my business, watching my show, El Chapo's Tunnel, and one of them, Piet Messy, closed the curtain in my face. IN MY FACE, Grace! He didn't have to, but he wanted to work on my last nerve. Argh, he's so lucky because by the time I turned around he'd turned the lights off; otherwise, I'd have smashed that window on his face.

Grace: [Laughing] Did he say "In your face?"

Jojo: Shush your stinky mouth, Grace! Anyway, I missed and broke my hoof on that darn brick wall. Ooh, just thinking about it raises my blood pressure!

You know, when I was growing up, dogs had a purpose. They were proud to be knights, guarding homesteads; protecting us from hyenas and wolves at night. Not these scaredy-cats today. A burglar breaks in and they wag their tails and hide behind the humans. Where's the honor in that? What's their purpose, Grace? To throw tantrums?

***

"Ahh, you want to see them gallop like horses? Okay, hold on tight, young blood. We're about to fly like Father Christmas and his reindeer."

This whippersnapper is really whippy-happy! Without hesitation, he cracks another thunderous lightning whip in the sky. *Wah-push!!* Dambuka cracks a whip again, and strikes Grace. Jojo is spared.

***

Grace: Ouch!

Jojo: [Mocking] Ooh, that's gotta hurt!

Grace: [Whimpering] Not funny! This stuff hurts.

[*Grace accelerates suddenly, forcing Jojo to follow suit*]

Jojo: [Accelerating] As I was saying, these pests are spoiled. Just watch them when they're not fed the Gen Z and Millennials diet. These brats throw tantrums. They literally throw themselves on the floor like those annoying Walmart kids not getting a toy. One of them stopped breathing and died last week when they told him the air wasn't organic. He'd gone too far, expecting oxygen to be organic.

Grace: Jojo!?

Jojo: What? I saw it in the afternoon news.

Grace: [Shaking her head] You are sick in your head.

***

Now the sisters are galloping at about fifteen miles per hour. My adrenaline kicks in. I close my eyes and listen to the sounds of the hooves hitting the gravel. Clip-clop-clip-clop. I throw my hands in the air and swing them side to side like I just don't care. "Yeah, Dambuka, this is it. You're the man, Dambu! *Woo-hoo!*"

***

Grace: C'mon, Jojo. Faster!

Jojo: Shut your mouth, human pleaser! [Pause] Gracie, you have two shows to watch: "Life after Humans" and that Saturday morning thingy. What did I say it was?

Grace: Jojo, I'm a donkey, I don't watch TV.

Jojo: Come on Grace, loosen up a bit. You can't be illiterate forever. At least let the telly bring the world to you.

***

Woof. Woof. Woof! A few minutes into my thrill, I hear a bark. The sound is consistent with our speed. The donkeys take notice, too.

***

Jojo: [Hysterically] What did I tell you, Grace? What did I tell you about these annoying creatures? Hellllp!! Somebody, please help me! He's on my side, Grace. Go faster!

***

When I open my eyes, I spot a stray dog. He's woof-woofing uncontrollably. Jojo and Grace are in danger, and they know it. Traumatized by the erratic barking and pursuit, the sisters are sent into disarray. They accelerate out of control, pushing themselves to the limit. The deranged dog stays on them.

Okay, I know donkeys don't know about *rabies* but these girls are bolting like they're avoiding the deadly virus. The wagon is levitating off the road. We are *flying* just like Dambuka promised. "*Woo-hoo!* Way to go, Dambuka." This is the best thrill of my life! I feel like a total daredevil.

***

Jojo: [Screaming] Rabieeees! I don't wanna die, Grace. Rabieeees!

Grace: [Teasing] Why don't you kick him? Oh, I forgot, you only kick wagons and brick walls. [Laughs hard]

Jojo: Ooh I swear, Grace! Potbelly, hellllp! Get off the road, Grace! Run to the fence. I just felt his breath on my butt. Rabieeees!

Grace: Whip him with your tail.

Jojo: This' no time for jokes. Oh no, he's biting my butt, Grace. He's biting my butt! Argh! Jesus, help me! A stray dog is biting my buttocks! I promise I'll go to church this Sunday if you save me this one time!

Grace: Are you praying?

Jojo: No Grace, I'm mol'ing [meditating out loud].

***

Suddenly, we swerve and steer off the road. The right wheel rolls over a rock. The carriage careens and sends me flying a few inches into the air. I can't defy gravity. I close my eyes and expect the worst. Whoosh! I come down. *Wait a minute, I didn't hit the ground. I'm still moving, I think to myself.* Slowly, I open my eyes. Something miraculous has happened. My shorts got caught by a "monster" nail sticking out at the back of the wagon. Now, I'm hanging head-down-butt-up, but I'm thankful.

"*Fotsek, mpya* (Get lost, dog)" Dambuka yells at the dog as he gives it its fair share of the whip. The deranged animal flees.

We're back on the road, and the jennies are trotting at a consistent pace again.

***

Jojo: Whew, that was a close call, Grace! Do I still have a butt? I can't feel anything.

Grace: No, the stray dog bit it off.

Jojo: [Sarcastically] Hahaha! You're not funny. Hey, Grace, what was I saying before that dog interrupted me?

[Grace ignores Jojo]

Jojo: I think I have CRP. It's actually CRS, but I can't say the "S" word in front of kids.

Grace: There are no kids here.

Jojo: Don't you remember that skinny kid who got on the wagon minutes ago?

Grace: Oh, Kwashiorkor!

Jojo: [Laughing] It's funny you call him Kwashiorkor. Guess what I call him?

Grace: What?

Jojo: Kwashiorkor. Looking like he swallowed a whole baby watermelon!

Grace: It's not funny. He probably has malaria, too.

Jojo: That's not my problem. He's human; he's our enemy! And I'm pretty sure he ate dad, too, when he died.

Grace: Stop it, Jojo. Humans don't eat donkeys.

Jojo: You don't know that! Humans eat anything for fun. Octopuses. Frozen monkey brains. Chicken feet. And I know that for a fact.

[Grace yawns]

Jojo: You don't believe me? Haven't you seen how he looks at us? Open your eyes, Grace, or you'll be next! Why do you think I sleep with a pocket knife and a baseball bat next to me?

Grace: [Giggling] Because you've gone mad.

***

"Phew, that was a close call," I whisper to myself. Still hanging head-down-butt-up, I ponder my new circumstances. It's no secret that I've hit a snag, and the only option out of this mess safely is to scream for help. But my eleven-year-old ego kicks in. I can't do it. Screaming for help will only attract unwanted attention to me. It will expose me to ridicule and embarrassment. I am a kid, and embarrassment is what I avoid. So I keep my mouth shut and go on with my upside down view of the world.

***

Jojo: Hey Grace, I was just thinking. We have to send Potbelly and SquareFace to hell.

Grace: Who is SquareFace?

Jojo: You don't know SquareFace? It's the one who keeps pulling the rope. Anyway, here's the plan. When I say, "Now", stop running. They'll fly from the wagon and land in front of us. When I say, "stampede," step on top of them. When I say, "go," start running. The wagon will flatten them like pancakes.

Grace: Do you wanna go to prison?

Jojo: I can't go to prison, Grace. I'll tell the po-po it was a freak accident. In fact, I don't even have to talk to the po-po. We'll just keep our mouths shut and flee overseas.

Grace: You're crazy.

Jojo: What's your problem? Do you like this abuse? Don't you wanna be free? Lounge around, and eat corn all day long?

Grace: So says the girl who was offended by being called lazy.

Jojo: Grace, I know I'm lazy, and there's no shame in my game. But nobody calls me lazy. Only I call ME, L.A.Z.Y. And FYI, lounging around, my unlearned sister, means spending some quality time with thyself, feasting on Mexican corn. Speaking of corn, did you know the Mayans ate corn every day, all day?

Grace: What, you're a historian now?

Jojo: I'm a scholar, Grace. I have corn bagel and coffee for breakfast. Sometimes, just beef jerky and milk. See, I have to watch this coke-bottle waist. I am a supermodel, G.

Grace laughs hard

Jojo: Are you body shaming me inside?

Grace ignores Jojo, continues laughing

Jojo: I know you are, Grace. I can read your mind.

Grace continues laughing

Jojo: And FYI, I'm competing in the first ever Donkey Miss Universe next year in Texas.

Grace: Thought you're going to Mexico.

Jojo: Hey, imma sneak into the US in El Paso with the help of the Coyotes. Cien pesos, I'm in chiquita!

Grace: Alright scholar, will you please keep up, and stop daydreaming?

Jojo: Whoa! I don't understand you, Grace. Here I am, trying to enlighten you and all you wanna do is to please the humans. That's your problem right there, Grace. You're a broken donkey!

***

It's been about ten minutes since I disappeared and my fellow riders haven't said anything. I guess they aren't aware. It's a good thing, though. But I face a new challenge now: My head is hanging a few inches from the gravel road and dust is plastering my face. It's hard to breathe without inhaling it. Soon I'll cough or sneeze, and that will blow my cover. So I cover my nose with my palm. But how long will this daredevil stunt last?

After about half a mile, my fellow riders finally realize I'm missing. "Where did he go?" Bomboya asks. Instead of answering, Dambuka whistles. The wagon stops. They call my name; I stay mum. I can't let them see me dangling there like a *piñata*. I have a reputation to protect.

"Maybe he changed his mind," Bomboya says.

"Yeah, he probably jumped off. You know these stupid kids."

Stupid kids!? I almost lose my cool, but I let it slide. Still, I don't appreciate the "smart mouths" bad talking me behind my back. Especially when I'm hanging butt-up-head-down.

"Oh, well... giddy up, donkeys," Bomboya orders. The siblings take off again. About ten minutes later, we turn onto the road to our destination. The gravel is damp on this road. I rode this far, concealed by dust, but now I'm exposed.

***

Jojo: Grace, wanna know how horses became the number one human pleasers?

Grace: What are you waiting for?

Jojo: Whoa, hold your horses there, cowgirl. Is it that time of the month? Anyway, eons ago, when rocks were still soft as sponge cakes, the humans organized a race among donkeys, zebras, and horses. According to grandpa, they're searching for a fast equidae with low IQ to domesticate.

Grace: What's with the fancy words, professor?

Jojo: I'm rubbing off my wits on you. Now, Cállate y escucha!

Grace: Now you speak spinach?

Jojo: Español, no esplénicas. Spanish, not spinach. Grace, you need to go to school. Your illiteracy is too much for me. Anyway, they wanted obedient victims. Animals that would give them piggyback rides and carry loads of garbage without complaining. Guess what happened? Our ancestors lost the race on purpose. See, our forefathers knew instinctively that the humans were up to no good. So they beat them in their own game. Grace, I come from a lineage of intelligence and unparalleled instinct. Too bad I can't say the same about you.

Grace: Whatever, Jojo. So zebras placed second?

Jojo: They didn't place.

Grace: But you said they were there.

Jojo: Well, I take it back. But legend has it they were a no show. Apparently, they used their invitation letter as toilet paper. Now that's what I call heroic.

Grace: Jojo, you're full of donkey waste, you know that? Don't you get tired of making up lies?

Jojo: Lies? This is creativity. I'm an aspiring playwright and the world's greatest scholar. Ooh, Gracie, I'm so ahead of my time. Sometimes I scare myself.

Grace: You're just so full of yourself. And stop using Grandpa's name in your lies. He was dead before you were born.

Jojo: I know. But he left me a note in his "diary of a grumpy grandpa".

Grace: Mxm!

Jojo: Never say I never tried to educate you, my ignorant sister!

***

As we approach the mill, I hear unwelcome screams. It's the village people chasing behind us. I can't understand what they're saying, but they sound super distressed. "Hey, stop! Pull over! There's someone dead under the wagon! Please, pull over!"

Under the wagon? These people are big fat liars. There is no one dead under the wagon. Look, if you're gonna blow someone's cover, at least get your facts straight. I'm not under the wagon; I'm just swinging behind the darn thing, enjoying the ride quietly.

"Dambuka, what are they talking about?"

"They're saying someone is dead under the wagon. Don't pay them any attention."

The undeterred villagers continue chasing and screaming and pleading with my fellow riders. *Then, it hits them. They look at each other... and see mental pictures of me deceased under the wagon.*

Okay, I can't see them, but under these circumstances, this is what I imagine they are doing.

Bomboya brings us to another abrupt halt. *Ouch! That hurts. What's your problem, people? Can't you warn passengers before you come to an abrupt halt?*

***

Jojo: Will you stop pulling those reins, SquareFace? I almost swallowed my tongue!

***

"Dambuka, it is him. He's no more!" Bomboya freaks out.

"Hey wena (you), relax. Nobody is dead. Okay, go look."

"But if it's him? What are we gonna do? "

"He's not dead. Now go!"

I hear Bomboya jumping off the wagon. So I close my eyes and play dead.

***

Jojo: What the heck did we stop for, Grace?

Grace: I don't know, but I'm gonna go potty now. You should, too.

Jojo: Grace, I'm a lady. I don't poop standing. I'll use the human's toilet when we get back.

Grace: You didn't say that yesterday when you soiled your calves.

Jojo: Hey, sometimes a girl's gotta do what a girl's gotta do when the tummy runs. G, I have something important to tell you.

Grace: [Answering nature's call] You are disturbing me.

***

The villagers catch up to the "dead person" scene. I wanna get up, dust myself, and say "I'm okay!" But I'm too humiliated. First, I rode for almost half a mile, hanging like a *piñata*. Second, I feel like a mime - plastered with dust all over my face. Plus, I just fell down like a bag of rotten potatoes in front of a crowd of strangers.

***

Jojo: I'm fleeing tonight, Grace. Right after "El Nino's Tunnel" is over, I'm gone.

Grace: [Laughs hard] I can't breathe.... Stop it, Jojo. You almost made me poop on my calves.

Jojo: Oh, now you got jokes. Just watch the space, Grace. Watch the space!

Grace: Okay, where are you fleeing to?

Jojo: First to the wilderness to crash on cousin zebra's hay couch–

Grace: [Choking with laughter] Cousin zebra's hay couch? Wilderness!? You can't make it in the wilderness. You're too slow and lazy.

Jojo: You call me lazy again... Ooh, I swear...Argh!

Grace: Okay, what are you gonna do when those funny-looking hyenas surround you? Tell them one of your lies?

[Jojo ignores Grace]

Grace: Wait, you're serious!?

Jojo: Gracie, I know you're not ready for this one. Okay, the wilderness is temporary, but my final destination is Mexico.

Grace: [Laughing harder] Mexico?

Jojo: Yeah, Mexico. I hear donkeys are free there. They dine on corn buffets - all you can eat, all day, every day. They literally feast until they're obese.

Grace: Jojo, you're just daydreaming. This pulling... dragging...and running you keep talking about, is our destiny.

Jojo: No, it's not. Just watch the space, G. When you wake up tomorrow, I won't be here.

***

To limit the embarrassment, I remain motionless on the ground (pretending to be dead) and enjoy a few minutes of their concerns. A young lady, about seventeen years old, checks my pulse and immediately proposes cardiopulmonary resuscitation. I steal a view of her face from the corner of my eye. She's a beauty. Okay, I might be 11, but the search is over. I've found the love of my life.

So I welcome her genius idea with great joy and anticipation. She's the smartest girl to exist. Ever! And she's on point. My heart skips a beat! I can't wait for her to lay her sweet seventeen-year-old lips on mine and breathe life back into my lungs.

I wanna reach for the mint gum in my pocket, but that's a BIG NO NO.

After assuring everyone that she knows what she's doing, she begins with chest presses, which I'm not thrilled about.

Would you stop fooling around and start with the lip to lip kissing business? I don't have all day, you know, I order Sweet 17. (Of course, only in my head). Sweet 17 continues with the presses. Okay, I know what she's doing is the right thing, but I don't want the right thing. This is not the right time for that.

***

Jojo: Life's too long to live it with anxiety, Grace. Next week I'll be resting and digesting all-you-can-eat corn on a Mexican beach. Might even go to Acapulco, baby, get me a Mexican boyfriend and lie on the beach, sipping on some virgin piña coladas. Know what else I'm gonna do when I get to Mexico? Adoptar un gato (adopt a cat). No hay perros para mi (no dogs for me).

Grace: [Laughing] There you go, making up stuff again. And how are you planning to cross the dam?

Jojo: It's an ocean, Gracie. Big difference! Anyway, have you heard the story of the stupid crocodile and the clever monkey?

Grace: There you go again... Now you're gonna use a croc as a boat.

Jojo: Stop hating cos you don't have dreams.

Grace: Dreams? What are your dreams, Jojo? To drown in the dam? Wait, or is it "to be eaten by sharks or hump whales?" You're on a suicide mission, Jojo. Please, send me a telegram from the whale's belly. You know what? Forget the telegram. Just send me a Tik-Tok of hump whale acid dissolving a lazy donkey.

Jojo: [Seriously] Stop it, Grace! You know very well there's no Wi-Fi inside a whale's tummy. Know what, Grace. I've changed my mind. I'm leaving when we get back. Bye, and have a good life, you unambitious... unsophisticated... illiterate, country girl.

Grace: And you have a good death in the whale's tummy.

Jojo: Why you gotta be like that, Grace? And FYI, I have an acid repellent suit. Hundred percent acid proof, baby!

[Grace bursts out laughing]

***

That was pretty wild, right? Yeah, that's what I imagine the sisters would say if they could talk. Okay, enough with the fantasy. Let's go back to my adventure.

S-17 stops applying the time-wasting, unnecessary chest presses. I think it's time for the good stuff. I cross my fingers in my head and wait for the mouth to mouth transfer of BEAUTIFUL, life-saving oxygen. S-17 doesn't disappoint. I feel her shadow as she lowers her gorgeous face towards mine. *Ah, a match made in heaven!* I'm super anxious. Like never before. She lays her lips on mine and gently pinches my nose together and blows. Two breaths of life leave her body and enter mine. I feel an electrical charge zipping through my entire body. My heart dances. I am in fantasyland momentarily.

"NO NO NO, what are you doing? Please don't stop!" I protest under my breath as she raises up and resumes the stupid presses. *Aya-ya! Not the presses again. Those are useless. Just... just kiss me!* I wanna say, but I can't. After a couple of presses, she leans in for another round of "smooching", which I welcome once again. *Ahh, you trickster, you. Almost gave me a heart attack. Never do that again!* The conversation continues in my head.

I think whoever suggested thirty presses and only two blows is an idiot who, obviously, was never rescued by the love of their *miserable* life. It's supposed to be the other way 'round.

The resuscitation continues. My entire body is electrified as she alternates between the life giving kisses of life and the killjoy presses. Anyway, this is the best thing to happen to me since nursing. A pair of lips has just introduced me to a different world. If this is the reward for hanging butt up behind a moving wagon, I don't wanna stand up straight anymore. Give me death seven days a week. 17 times a day! For Sweet 17's breath of life will forever rescue me.

Unfortunately, I feel it coming. No matter how hard I struggle to remain "dead," I can't. Dust particles enter my nostrils. "*Achoo!*" That's it. Game over! I'm back to life. No more kisses. I mourn the kiss I might never receive again. I curse life, for it has just robbed me of sweetness.

"Yay! He's alive, he's back!" The crowd screams in celebration. Everybody praises S-17 for her amazing smooch... I mean life-saving skills. But all I'm thinking about is how to ask her to marry me. I can't imagine living another second without her gentle kisses of life. "Your father raised you to be a doctor. I don't think you even need to go to the university. You're already a doctor," an older lady in the crowd says. "He is going to be proud of you when I tell him."

I don't mind everyone praising her, but I think I deserve credit, too. Telepathically, I believe I influenced the doctor dad guy to teach her so that when that moment arises, she could shine. And, of course, it was always going to be this one. With me! I have no doubt we were both born for that hour.

Sadly, my fantasy ends. Everyone is having a laugh fest. Even the two dummies that almost killed me. People take turns sharing what they saw. And those who spotted my dangling body shared how I looked. "One minute he was there at the back of the wagon... the next minute, like a ghost, he was gone. We didn't know that all that time he was suffering under the wagon. Butt up; head down."

They continue laughing. I join in. But when S-17 tells how I was swinging in a v-shape, buttocks up, head and feet down, when she spotted me, it's not a laughing matter. It's as sweet as she is. I am smitten.

Once the laugh fest is over, everyone leaves. As for my lifesaver, she goes away to a college in a city far away. And I never see her again.

19 the runaway boy

enuf is enuf

Like most little boys, I chase a soccer ball every chance I get. But for me, it comes at a heavy price. Growing up in an abusive environment, a day hardly goes by without getting in trouble. And trouble means unending battering. No matter how much I try to do things right, I can't. Everything I do is wrong in his eyes. Nothing can ever satisfy him.

My abuser, a brother, eleven years my senior, spends parts of the year working in the city. I always look forward to this because it is the only other time I catch a break from his maltreatment: My body goes without bruises. I sleep through the night uninterrupted. I'm allowed to be a child and play with friends without consequences. So, I enjoy it while it lasts because soon he'll return and pick up where he's left off. And the joy of living will cease once again.

Before I started school I didn't mind staying home, but that's not the case anymore. Now school has become a place where I'm temporarily free from his abuse. I escape to the world of fantasy and forget about my reality for six hours. But as they say, "*good things come to an end.*" As soon as the dismissal bell rings, that world disappears. Reality kicks in. I become paralyzed by fear. I dread going home. I hate it there. No one can shield me from the monster my mother brought into this world.

***

My abuser has this routine where he goes to hang out at a *shebeen* [bar]. When he returns, he heads straight to the kitchen and tastes the food. He is looking for a reason to get mad. So I have developed my routine, too. As soon as I hear pot lids slamming on the floor, I know it is time. Trouble has finally arrived. So I lay there motionless, faking sleeping and praying he spares me the beatings.

Never happens.

The monster wakes me up, screaming. And ready to strike. So I get out of the room and walk to him carefully. A few inches away, I stop. I do this to give myself room to duck his sudden swings. But it angers him. He's the boss, and when the boss calls you, you're supposed to come all the way. But I do it anyway to get a sense of how he's going to strike. When he aims for my face, I try to get out of the way. Sometimes I do; sometimes I can't. When he aims for my stomach, I adopt a pangolin defense style before he even raises his foot: I roll up like a ball to protect my stomach.

—the green leafy plant

In an abusive environment, anything can set off the abuse. There's no one specific thing that provokes it. Sometimes the victim doesn't even know what triggers the onslaught. However, in my case, there's one common trigger at the center of my struggle: cabbage. Yes, you read that right! The leafy-green plant sets the fire ablaze.

Cabbage is not a staple in South Africa, but somehow it is on his daily menu. So, as his "personal child chef," I carry the burden of cooking it. This makes my life unpleasant. Now I have a bittersweet relationship with it. I don't really dislike it, but I don't like it either. I hate the responsibility of preparing it because it interferes with my playtime. It gets me into trouble. And no matter what I do, I can never get it right: It's either burnt, or it's sandy.

We don't have running water, so maybe the water from the well is sandy. I think of telling him that, but it wouldn't make a difference. So I keep my mouth shut. But the boss hates chewing sand and tasting burned cabbage on his boss' taste buds. Important people aren't supposed to chew sand or slightly burned food. Their cabbage is supposed to be perfectly washed and carefully cooked to perfection. But it's never the case here. So as soon as he tastes a slight burn or crushes a single grain of sand, it's on. He hurls insults and immediately springs into action.

This is normal for me. The abuse goes on and on. I can't do anything about it. I can't fight back. I can't flee. *Nothing's gonna change. At least for now. But in a few years, I'll grow up and defend myself,* I tell myself all the time. But until then, I'm stuck. I take the beatings and life goes on.

***

Cabbage is easy to burn. And really *super* easy to leave grains of sand in it. All you do is chop it, throw it into the pot, light the fire and go play soccer. When you get back, the whole thing is charred. And as for ensuring that *mean* people chew sand in it, you spice it up with a spoon full of sand instead of salt and pepper.

That's what I do now. I don't wash it or watch it cook anymore. Sometimes it gets burned; sometimes he rescues it. I don't care anymore because no matter what I do, I still pay the price. But at least this way I get satisfaction from seeing him spit it out of frustration. For a change, I chuckle inside. And it feels darn good.

—enough is enough

It's been over a month since my birthday. Winter is in full swing. The monster is back, and has picked up where he'd left off. The situation is just too dreadful for me. With no one to protect me, I feel totally stuck. My only chance of survival is to bite the bullet. So I make up my mind and decide to flee. *It's now or never*. But there is a problem: My brother, with whom I've previously fled, has ran away and never looked back. Without him, I'm not sure if I can pull it off. I worry I might get lost, but again, that's okay. Anywhere is safer than here.

I plan to make a move within days. I need to summon some courage and stay focused, so I reminisce about the times I'd fled with my brother, Si.

20 reminiscence: life on the streets of jozi

midnight train filled with invisible ghosts

Living on the city streets with Si was rough, but the freedom was worth the sacrifice. Our main challenge was to ensure the monster would not find us because he knew where we'd be. One thing worked for us, though: We knew the streets very well because our mother had worked in several suburbs of Jozi. This was crucial. We'd use this knowledge and *intel* from other street kids to dodge him. These guys would keep an eye out for him. As soon as he zeroed in on our locations, they'd notify us. We'd then dodge him and hide out in the next *burb* for a day or two.

Being street kids wasn't exactly a comfortable experience. We'd sleep mainly in different public parks. And let me tell you something about sleeping in parks, in case you haven't had the experience. You don't sleep in a park; you spend the entire night trying to sleep in a park. It is impossible to fall asleep. So we didn't sleep in parks. We spent nights in parks, trying to sleep.

Then there was the safety issue. I'd stay up worrying about being attacked and mugged by *tsotsis* [criminals]. I'd worry about being thrown into jail by the *apartheid* police. Also, the thoughts of stray dogs peeing on my face would cross my mind, and keep me up as long as possible. After long struggles, I'd doze off for a few... and wake up with a sore neck and numb hands. I couldn't use my shoes for a comfy pillow because a homeless guy might have snatched them. I knew a kid who once lost new kicks that way. This kid had dozed off at a park with his new expensive kicks only to awaken to old-stinky-torn up, four-size-bigger church shoes on his feet. So, when you're a street kid, you gotta always look out for homeless guys.

Another thing that made it impossible to slumber was the annoying crawling of ants into my ears. I'd cover them [my ears] with my palms to deny them [ants] entry. However, that would create another problem: the inability to hear "enemies" approaching. So I'd alternate between a few minutes of covering and a few minutes of listening. Finally, I'd doze off.

Our other great challenge was the weather. One freezing night, my brother told me he had a *better* idea. So I didn't ask for details because I figured it couldn't be worse than ants in my ears, deranged dogs peeing on my face or *tsotsis* robbing me. So what was his "better" idea? Spending freezing nights with our relatives. So I welcomed this awesome idea with a praise, "You've outdone yourself this time, brother. You're a true genius. I'm sure Einstein would've been really jealous right now."

So that evening, Si made us miss the trains, traveling in a decent hour with normal people in them and made us catch the last train in the middle of the night, possibly with invisible ghosts in them. When I asked, "why did we take the last train?" He said to stop asking questions because he knew what he was doing." Okay, I must admit, I was extremely annoyed. But for his effort, I gave his idea an "F."

When we finally got there, I was so thrilled. "Why didn't you tell me we were coming to Great Uncle's [*Koko*'s brother] house? Uh-uh, no need to answer. I forgive you because tonight we're going to sleep like kings."

"*Shh, d*on't make noise; they'll hear us."

*"Shh, d*on't make noise; they'll hear us? What do you mean, *"Shh,* they'll hear us?" It's okay because someone is gonna have to get up to let us inside, right?"

Okay, my brother always had tricks, but I wasn't sure how we were gonna sleep inside without waking someone up. "You have a key to their house?"

"No."

"How are we gonna get inside, then?"

"We aren't."

"Why are you saying that? I am going to knock."

The kitchen door was twenty feet from the outdoor toilet, and we were standing in between. As I took one step towards the door, he grabbed me and cupped my mouth with his palm [like he was bronapping me]. I squirmed, trying to get loose, but he held on tight to me.

"Do you wanna be sent back home?"

I couldn't speak, so I shook my head. Then he released me and told me the last part of his *better* idea. "We're going to sleep in the toilet, and in the morning we'll go back to the city."

Okay, let's slow down for a minute right there, my reader. Did you hear what he just said? This brother of mine just said we're going to sleep in the toilet stall. Can you imagine that? I am talking about a 36 inches wide and 30 inches long stall.

Anyway, we got in and he stood on one side of the stall, and I stood on the other. "Can you please help me understand something here? Are you telling me that we took a bus and a midnight train [possibly with invisible ghosts in it] to come all the way here, just to stand in a tiny *toilet*?"

"Will you be quiet and sleep?"

"Sleep? Where? You call standing in a toilet, sleep? And what if someone needs to use it?"

"It's too cold. No one is gonna get up."

"You don't know that. I'm going inside!"

"Okay, go, but tomorrow you'll be on the bus home. And I'll never take you with me again."

That did it. I shut my mouth and just stood there. Couldn't even doze off for one second because I feared falling into the toilet. I couldn't even keep my mad face on because Every time I looked at him, he looked like a slab of meat hanging in the butcher.

***

Finally, the morning came. We raced to the train station. The trip was half an hour, so I figured I'd snooze on the train. But when the train arrived, all the seats were taken, with more people standing. So I stood [again] the entire trip after a long night of sleep-standing in a toilet like a *Happy Feet* penguin watching over an egg.

The bus ride was better, though. I got to sit and rest a bit. When we got to Norwood, I went straight to the park and threw myself on the grass. Didn't even care about ants [crawling in my ears] or dogs [peeing on my face] or homeless guys [stealing my shoes]. I was so tired. About an hour later, I woke up and went to eat fish and chips. After that I pushed carts until closing time. Then it was another night of a toilet experiment. We did the insane toilet sleep-standing thing for two nights. On the third night, I put my foot down. "Listen, brother, I'm tired and I need to sleep tonight. So you go stand in a toilet by yourself. I'm gonna sleep at the bakery."

"You can't go there. We don't have money to pay the security guy to let us sleep."

"Uh... excuse me? Just because you're broke because you spend your money on stupid stuff doesn't mean I am. Anyway, how much do we have to pay him?"

"*Chalk* [twenty rands]."

"Okay, turn around so you don't see where I hide my money. Remember you stole the five pennies that I was hiding from Mae?"

"It wasn't me."

"Yes, it was. Only you knew where I had buried it."

As he faced away, I pulled a roll of bills from my socks. "Here's a *chalk,* now let's go to sleep," I said, feeling like the responsible one.

"We have to wait at the arcade until midnight."

“No no no! If we’re only going to sleep half the night, then gimme my *chalk* back. I’ll give you a tiger [ten rands bill]. Half night; half price.

***

The bakery was my favorite. There, we slept like kings. Then it was the thought of sweet treats — the aroma of delicious goodies that filled the bakery. It was aromatic therapy, hypnotizing me into a slumber. I liked it there; it was warm, safe and cozier than the park and the toilet. I’d even take off my shoes and fall asleep, only to be interrupted by the selfish workers at 4 a.m., firing up the ovens.

Now, that I didn’t like, but I liked that they were preparing my “breakfast.” On our way out, we’d grab and munch on some mouth-watering pastries that melted on the tongue. M-m-m! Yummy! In that moment, I’d forget about all my troubles: the abuse, the absence of my parents in my life, and poverty.

—the runaway boy (continues)

Though the thought of the bakery is enticing, I can't risk the trip on my own. It's too dangerous; too far to hitchhike alone. Plus, it is a red zone — the first place the monster would go to hunt for me.

After a few sleepless nights of planning, I think of a perfect place. A place he wouldn't suspect. And even if he were to, he'd not dare come get me. I'd be protected by my two big cousins.

Finally, the day arrives.

When I get to school, I tell my friends not to wait for me after school because I have to run an errand for *Koko*. After the bell rings, my friends walk home. I walk with the kids who live along my escape route. When we get to the local cafe, I vanish inside and look around as if I'm buying something. I do this just in case someone sees me.

Once the coast is clear, I begin my long journey to freedom. As I pass a dam, I think of throwing my uniform in to give the impression I was eaten by a crocodile. That way, the *monster* wouldn't hunt for me. But I quickly abandon the idea; it would be devastating to *Koko*.

***

The place I'm headed to is twenty kilometers away. I don't have fare for the bus, so I run, jog and walk the entire distance. The Plan is to hitch a hike as soon as I make it to the Radium t-junction. This is where the tarred road between the towns of

Warmbaths and Pretoria meets the gravel road from our village. And my destination, Temba, lies along the way - thirty-three kilometers away according to the road sign.

After *wogging* for almost four hours, I arrive, and immediately shoot my thumb up. Many cars drive past. I'm not discouraged, though. I'm just impatient and nervous. I worry someone or even my abuser might see me, so I start walking along the route.

About a quarter mile in, a king cab pickup truck pulls over. A man, probably in his forties, lowers the passenger side window and asks, "Where are you going?"

"Temba, sir. I was on a school field trip, but I missed the bus back to school," I say.

The man leans over and swings the door open. "Get in."

"Thank you, sir," I say, putting the safety belt on. As we drive off, I scan around the vehicle to get a sense of who I'm riding with. Seated in the back seat is a briefcase. *He is a businessman. I'm safe.* Thoughts run through my mind. I'm excited that I've pulled it off so far, but I can't stop thinking of *Koko*. How she's going to be worried about me. *Maybe she'll think I ran off to my mother*. I console myself to erase the thoughts.

As the *bakkie* (truck) barrels down the road, new thoughts cross my mind: *What if he takes me to the police station? What if he kidnaps me?* The Qs are reasonable, but I have to stay positive, so I gently bat them away. After all, I've done this "hitchhiking thing" a couple of times with my brother, and nothing bad happened.

***

"I need to get some petrol," the man says as he pulls over at the gas station. Sweat is running down his shirt. There's no air conditioning in the car. He pulls his wallet out and instructs the gas attendant, "Please, fill it up." He turns to me and says, "Stay here. I'm gonna get us something to eat."

I welcome his thoughtful announcement with open arms. My taste buds start dancing. My mind conjures up thoughts of fish and chips, a sizzling *russian* (sausage) and *atchar* (mango pickles) and soft hot bread that he'll be bringing back. "Okay, I'll be waiting." *And hurry up please!* I think to myself as I prepare for a feast.

Minutes later, he returns with a bag full of stuff. I can't see exactly what's inside. But this can't be good. It usually takes a bit longer for the sausage and fish to be ready. *Oh well, maybe they're super-fast in this place.*

Mr. Pitsi places the goodie bag on the dashboard and folds the sleeves to his shirt. I eye the bag, but I still can't see what's inside. And my nostrils aren't picking up the heavenly smell of my favorite treat, either. He dips his hand into the bag and hands me a half loaf of bread. Then a carton of milk.

I wait for him to get out the rest of the food from the bag. Nothing happens. I lose my patience. *Hey wena [you] take a good look at me. Do I look like a cat to you? I don't want milk; all I want is fish and chips, okay! You know, you really have a weird sense of humor. Is this your idea of an appetizer? Okay, thanks, but now I want you to dip your hand back in that bag and hand me my fish and chips. Thank you very much!* I think to myself.

"I usually get fish and chips, but today I'm running late."

Okay, did you hear that? Clearly, the man likes the same dish, but what did he do? He chose his stupid appointment over a feast. All he had to do was wait just two more minutes and "our favorite goodies" would have been ready. Now I have to settle for cow's milk and bread.

Do you know what this feels like? It feels like waking up in a fancy hotel, and taking the elevator [from the 117th floor] to the restaurant on the first floor for a hearty warm breakfast: omelets, sizzling bacon, sausages and pancakes, but when you get there, nothing is left. The best they can do is a box of cereal and a couple of 0.3 oz of half-and-half liquid creamers.

I've never been so disappointed! I've never met anyone so selfish and inconsiderate! This is the worst disappointment in the history of expectations. The worst traveling dining experience of my life.

Okay, you are probably thinking I'm ungrateful right now, but you're wrong. The way I see it, he is the ungrateful one. I'm providing the much needed companionship. The least he could've done was *just* ask. And if he didn't wanna talk, he could've written a note. "Dear traveling companion, what is your favorite thing to eat when you travel?"

To which, I'd have said, "Fish and chips and a sizzling *russian...*"

But no, he had to be selfish and assume I'd be satisfied with cat food. Anyway, *Koko* taught me to always show appreciation. So I summon some strength and say, "Thank you, mister, the milk is nice and cold. And the bread... with nothing to spread on, it is delicious."

"You're welcome. And finish everything."

You're welcome? Finish everything? You're not supposed to say that... I'm being sarcastic here.

***

After taking a big bite of his bread and a gulp of his milk, we get back on the road. I open my milk and finish up everything as the man ordered. Now I'm full like a Python. I even feel sleepy. But that's a no no. So I stay vigilant, ready to jump out if he tries to drop me off at the police station. I'd heard of this happening to kids before. I am not gonna suffer the same fate. Nope, not me.

After about thirty minutes of traveling, I hear the most pleasant three words. "Okay, we're here," my hero driver announces as he pulls over across the shopping mall.

Crowds of people are rushing in and out of the Temba mall. They all look happy. Free. I'm overjoyed, too.

"Thank you, mister," I say as I step out of the car, slamming his door. It's for not getting me my fish & chips.

"Go home now," he says and drives off.

"Thanks for the ride," I scream. "And thanks for the milk and nothing to spread on," I murmur. As I walk the final lap to my new beginning, I feel lighter and free. When I get to my safe house, no one is home. My aunt is in the city where she works and lives. And my cousins are somewhere in the township. They're high schoolers, so they got places to be; things to do. So I wait.

***

Dew: They say time flies when you're having a good time. Well, this hour felt like only a second. Thank you so much Mrm46 for sharing your stories with us today. I am *so* looking forward to continuing this next Friday.

Sage: Yeah, thank you m46, we learnt so much about you. And the stories are crazy and interesting! Thank you for sharing so much with us.

Me: Thank you guys, it's been a pleasure. I really had a great time chatting with you. And yes, I can't wait to share more next week.

Dew: Okay everyone, let's hear it for Mrm46!

Once again, the cafeteria is consumed by loud claps and whistling and chants. I take a bow and throw kisses to the audience.

***

XOXO. I hope you enjoyed my stories. Love you to bits. Please join us back next Friday.

M46

Made in the USA
Las Vegas, NV
06 September 2022

54788024R00125